The Priesthood, Mystery of Faith

The Priesthood, Mystery of Faith

*Priestly Ministry in the
Magisterium of John Paul II*

Nilson Leal de Sá, CB

Foreword by Cardinal José Saraiva Martins

The Catholic University of America Press
Washington, D.C.

Originally published in Portuguese as *O sacerdócio : « mistério da fé »*. *O ministério presbiteral no magistério de São João Paulo II*, São José dos Campos, Editora ComDeus, 2018.

The paper used in this publication meets the minimum requirements of American National Standards for Information Science—Permanence of Paper for Printed Library Materials, ANSI Z39.48–1984.

∞

Cataloging-in-Publication Data available from the Library of Congress
Paperback ISBN: 978-0-8132-3508-0
Ebook ISBN: 978-0-8132-3509-7

Imprimatur: Most Reverend Samuel J. Aquila, S.T.L.
Archbishop of Denver
Denver, Colorado, USA
September 17, 2019

"Oh, miracle—
thus to be able to give
what we ourselves do not possess,
sweet miracle of our empty hands!"

Georges Bernanos, *Diary of a Country Priest*
(London: Boriswood, 1937), 194.

To my friends and brother priests.

Table of Contents

Foreword

Upon his election to the See of Peter, Pope Benedict XVI invited the whole Church to collect the rich doctrinal, spiritual, and pastoral heritage of his predecessor. But in this heritage, which engages the ordinary pontifical magisterium, the reflection on the priestly ministry occupies an important place. And this book that I have the joy of prefacing, presents itself as a real and stimulating synthesis of John Paul II's thought about the ministerial priesthood, at least as it emerges from the corpus of twenty-seven letters to priests written on the occasion of Holy Thursday.[1]

A few months before being elected pope, Cardinal Wojtyła had written a remarkable article for the formators of the candidates to the priesthood entitled "Holiness as a priestly identity card"[2] and published in the magazine *Seminarium*. This lifelong program of holiness consists of the deepest integration of the priest's identity and mission. A good and solid doctrinal knowledge of this vocation, this identity, and this mission is at the service of this "unity of life" well emphasized by the Decree of the Second Vatican Council on the ministry and the life of the priest.[3]

The title of this volume, "The Priesthood, Mystery of Faith," judiciously borrowed from the penultimate *Letter to Priests* of John Paul II (2004), is fortunately chosen in many ways. On the one hand, because it reflects the familiarity of the author with the thought of John Paul II who, on the occasion of the fiftieth anniversary of his priestly ordination, wished to share the memories of and reflections on his own vocation as a priest in a book entitled *Gift and Mystery* (1996). On the other hand, because it is truly in eminent fidelity to the *fidei depositum* (the deposit of faith) to which the pontifical magisterium of John Paul II testifies, offering to all, priests, laypeople, consecrated—in the light of the Holy Scriptures and of the Living Tradition—a deeper understanding *sub lumen fidei* (under the light of faith) regarding the intelligence of the inestimable gift that God makes to the whole Church through the sacrament of the Holy Orders. In this matter, as in many others, John Paul II was like a "head of a household who brings from his storeroom both the new and the old" (Mt 13:52).

---

1 From now on each *Letter to Priests for Holy Thursday* will be designated by the word *Letter*, followed by its year of publication and the number (abbreviated to "no.") of the cited paragraph.

2 Karol Wojtyła, "La sainteté sacerdotale comme carte d'identité," *Seminarium* 1 (1978): 167–81.

3 Cf. *Presbyterorum Ordinis*, 14.

In his last book, entitled *Memory and Identity*, Pope John Paul II magnificently states: "The Church is, in a certain sense, the 'living memory' of Christ: of the mystery of Christ, of his passion, death, and resurrection, of his Body and Blood. This 'memory' is accomplished through the Eucharist. It follows that Christians, as they celebrate the Eucharist in 'memory' of their Master, continually discover their own identity."[4]

How much more this is true for the priests called to utter the words of Christ at the altar: "Do this in memory of me" (Lk 22:19; 1 Cor 11:24)! The chapters of this book on the identity of the priest as "memory of Christ" are part of this perspective and are best able to accurately reflect the theological articulations of the thought of John Paul II.

We are particularly grateful to the author of this book for having been able to highlight with great care and nuance the Marian dimension of the ministerial priesthood so dear to John Paul II. Indeed, the whole magisterium of John Paul II has shone forth in all its radiance this dimension of priestly ministry, based on the special link that exists between the ministerial priesthood and the mother of the high priest associated with his work of Redemption: "All the superhuman experience of the sacrifice of our redemption, engraved in the Heart of the Mother of Christ the Redeemer— was entrusted to the man who received the Cenacle, the power to make this sacrifice present through the priestly ministry of the Eucharist."[5]

If it is true that Jesus gives his mother to all men without exception, He gives her to them by giving her first to the priests. Addressing them with a letter on the importance of women in the life of the priest, Pope John Paul II was careful to reaffirm it: "If the priesthood is by its nature ministerial, we must live it in union with the Mother who is the Handmaid of the Lord. Then our priesthood will be kept safe in her hands, indeed in her heart, and we shall be able to open it to everyone. In this way our priesthood, in all its dimensions, will be fruitful and salvific."[6]

By entrusting and dedicating priests to the Immaculate Heart of Mary in Fatima on May 12, 2010, Pope Benedict XVI effected a crucial act that is in profound continuity with the magisterium of his predecessor, Saint John Paul II. May this book help to make this magisterium better known for the glory of God and the salvation of souls.

Cardinal José Saravia Martins
Prefect Emeritus of the Congregation for the Causes of Saints

---

4 Pope John Paul II, *Memory and Identity* (London: Weidenfeld & Nicolson, 2005), 144–45.
5 *Letter* 1998, no. 3.
6 *Letter* 1995, no. 8.

Abbreviations

AA	Decree on the Apostolate of Laity *Apostolicam actuositatem*
AG	Decree on the Mission Activity of the Church *Ad gentes*
CD	Decree concerning the Pastoral Office of Bishops *Christus Dominus*
CCC	Catechism of the Catholic Church
DS	H. Denzinger, A. Schönmetzer, ed., *Enchiridion Symbolorum, definitionum et declarationum de rebus fidei et morum*
GS	Pastoral Constitution on the Church *Gaudium et spes*
LG	Dogmatic Constitution on the Church *Lumen gentium*
OT	Decree on Priestly Training *Optatam totius*
Per.	*Periodica de re morali canonica liturgica* 1920–1990; after 1991, *Periodica de re canonica*
PDV	Post-Synodal Apostolic Exhortation *Pastores dabo vobis*
PG	*Patrologiae cursus completus, Series graeca*, I-CLXI, ed. J. P. Migne, Paris 1844–1864
PL	*Patrologiae cursus completus, Series latina*, I-CCXXI, ed. J. P. Migne, Paris 1844–1864
PO	Decree on the Ministry and Life of Priests *Presbyterorum ordinis*
SC	Constitution on the Sacred Liturgy *Sacrosanctum concilium*

Introduction

"[The] mystery of faith is also the priesthood itself." This expression, which inspired the title of this work, is taken from the penultimate *Letter to Priests* of Saint John Paul II, dated March 24, 2004. It is with this exclamation that we see him close the long series of letters that he faithfully addressed to the priests every year on the occasion of Holy Thursday since the beginning of his pontificate. After having written many pages on the priesthood and its different aspects, this is what he still wanted to affirm: the priesthood is a mystery of faith!

When on October 16, 1978, Karol Wojtyła, then Cardinal Archbishop of Krakow, was elected successor to the chair of Saint Peter, the Catholic Church was still just beginning to fully integrate the Second Vatican Council into her life. He recognized "that the years following the council, for all their undoubted wealth of beneficial leaven, [. . .] have also seen the occurrence of a crisis and the appearance of not a few rifts" within the ecclesial body.[1] The understanding of the ministerial priesthood does not escape the assessment: it is deeply touched by the crisis, both in the context of its developments inside the Church and by social transformations. The result is a serious questioning of the identity of the ordained minister.

Karol Wojtyła was, during the conciliar sessions, one of the most vigorous promoters of the laity, of their vocation to holiness and of their own mission within the People of God.[2] This rediscovery of the lay faithful, of their vocation and mission in the Church, as well as the conciliar affirmation of the equal dignity of all the baptized, is in a certain way the backdrop to the questions surrounding the ordained priesthood. To this has been added the scarcity of priests and priestly vocations. Furthermore, more emphasis was given to new pastoral practices that entrusted laypeople with certain ecclesial services. In the face of this situation, a question arose: what is the specificity of the priestly ministry? The Holy Thursday letters seemed to formulate an appropriate response, full of faith and hope. I undertook this work, marveling above all before the mystery of the priesthood. Is it not

---

1 *Letter* 1982, no. 6.

2 Cf. George Weigel, *Witness to Hope: The Biography of Pope John Paul II* (New York: Harper Perennial, 1999), 160–66.

surprising that priests are given the task of having a piece of bread and a little wine become the Body and Blood of Our Lord? Likewise, with what fear and respect can it be said, "I absolve you from your sins," while the priest experiences his own sins and knows that only God can forgive them?[3] Also, how can he be proud when, in his being, one seeks to find above all the man of God, an expert in His Word, and dispenser of His sacraments? Furthermore, it is in the service of this "mystery of faith" that in Europe, Africa, and Asia I devoted myself for seventeen years to priestly formation.

But beyond this heartfelt reason there is, one could say, an intellectual reason at stake. Indeed, after almost twenty-seven years of his pontificate, what was John Paul II's legacy regarding the ministerial priesthood? What answers did he give to the questions still surrounding this reality today? The task and the volume of texts on this topic were immense, and I had to limit my field of study. So, the main source was finally chosen as the twenty-seven letters of Holy Thursday,[4] addressed annually to the priests.

In interviews with Cardinal Georges-Marie Cottier, theologian emeritus of the Pontifical House and thereby a connoisseur of the texts of the Holy Father, I realized that this choice was appropriate. Thus, he assured me with certainty that "the Letters of Holy Thursday were written by John Paul II himself." This affirmation has validated my conviction that I would analyze original texts. Historically and critically, it seemed fundamental: letters to priests were born of a personal initiative, where the pope spoke *ab imo pectore* (from the depths of his heart), giving a little of himself and his thought.

Another enlightening meeting was that with Cardinal Albert Vanhoye, an eminent specialist on the Epistle to the Hebrews. The opportunities for

---

3 Cf. Mk 2:7; Lk 5:21.

4 In this main source I included three homilies: 1) the homily of the Chrism Mass, April 16, 1981, because that year the pope did not send a letter for Holy Thursday; 2) the homily at the World Jubilee of Priests, February 23, 1984, since it is this text that the pope addressed to the priests that year; 3) the homily of the Chrism Mass, April 17, 2003, since he sent his encyclical *Ecclesia de Eucharistia* as a letter to priests. The source documents also include the letter *Dominicae Cenae* to the bishops of the Church on the Mystery and Worship of the Eucharist (February 24, 1980), usually labelled *Letter* 1980 in keeping with the other letters cited.

For those looking to find the original texts, it should be noted that only some prior to 1992 are available in English at https://www.vatican.va/content/john-paul-ii/en/letters.index.html, although most are available in other languages such as Spanish (except 1985, 1989, and 1990). A complete collection in print is found in *Letters to My Brother Priests* (Downers Grove, IL: Midwest Theological Forum, 2006). Another frequently cited set of documents in this study is a series of general audience that the pope gave on the priesthood in 1993; for a complete list of my sources, see the bibliography at the end of the book.

exchange and correction of my findings allowed me to understand the priestly figure of Christ who expresses Himself, and the use that John Paul II made of this epistle, which was so important for him. Thus, one is able to perceive how the pope, starting with the image of Christ the Sovereign Priest, deepens the knowledge of the priestly ministry. For John Paul II, the mystery of the Incarnation of the Son of God is the essential element of Divine Revelation, which enables us to understand the ministerial priesthood.

With those clarifications and stimulations to my research, I have sought in the diversity of the letters of Holy Thursday the major points of the thought of John Paul II. A careful reading of these writings has given rise to three chapters, which are an attempt to answer the initial question about his magisterium on ordained ministry within the context of his pontificate. Thus, the first chapter dwells on the sources of his teaching and emphasizes his use of the Word of God, Tradition, and the conciliar Magisterium. These foundations are the basis of the second chapter, in which I wanted to highlight the priestly identity in the life of the Church. Finally, the first two chapters yield to a third chapter on the specific mission of the priest.

Chapter 1

The Sources of John Paul II

THE WORD OF GOD:
JOHN PAUL II INTERPRETS THE LETTER TO THE HEBREWS

The scriptural sources of John Paul II are very numerous. Indeed, one finds in his letters a large number of quotations and references to the New Testament: the Synoptic Gospels, the writings of Saint John (Gospel, Epistles, and Apocalypse), the Epistles of Saint Peter and especially of Saint Paul,[1] and the Letter to the Hebrews. Some quotes from the Old Testament (Genesis, the Psalms, and the prophet Isaiah) are also found.[2]

In his letters, the pope dealt with various themes related to the priestly ministry, in its doctrinal as well as its pastoral dimensions, such as identity, formation, celibacy, prayer, sacraments, friendship with Christ, women, family, youth, catechesis, vocations, and holiness. On these occasions, the Word of God is often used, particularly to illustrate the subject treated as it is developed in his personal reflection.[3]

It would be difficult to analyze the usage of each quote, or at least the most frequently quoted in the letters.[4] However, it is good to consider at this point his selection of the Letter to the Hebrews. This choice is justified by the importance that the pope himself gives to this epistle: according to the Holy Father, "the Letter to the Hebrews [is] a fundamental text for knowledge

---

1 Above all, there are epistles to the Corinthians, Galatians, Ephesians, Philemon, Colossians, Timothy, and Romans.

2 Especially Isaiah 61:1–3, on the anointing of the Messiah: "The Spirit of the Lord God is upon me, because the Lord has anointed me."

3 Thus, to illustrate this point, in the *Letters* of 1983 and 2002, which deal with the Sacrament of Penance, besides the texts usually used for this sacramental subject, John Paul II uses quotations under the prism of the Sacrament of Reconciliation (Jn 6:51; Ps 130[129]:7; 2 Cor 5:19; Lk 19:1–10); the *Letter* 1988 is imbued with Marian spirituality, and the texts chosen expressly wish to highlight, for example, the "resemblance" between the maternity of Mary and that of the priests (cf. Gal 4:19; Is 49:15); the relationship with women is particularly developed in his *Letter* 1995, where the pope supports his reflections with texts such as Gn 1:27, 2:24, and 1 Cor 7:7, among others. The pope finds in the Word of God an essential source of his thought.

4 Of course, the references to the institution of the Eucharist often come back: Mk 14:22–25; Mt 26:26–28; Lk 22:19–20; 1 Cor 11:23–25.

of Christ's and our own priesthood."[5] Starting from a set of quotations and references, John Paul II offers a meditation on the priesthood of Christ and the ministerial priesthood that I wish to present in three parts: "Jesus Christ, our only high priest," "Vocation and service," and "Priest for eternity."

Jesus Christ, our Only High Priest

A first claim, crucial and notable, that emerges from the reflection of John Paul II in support of the Letter to the Hebrews is the reference to Christ as high priest.

> The Letter to the Hebrews expresses this truth most completely, referring to Christ as "high priest of the good things that have to come," who "entered once for all into the Holy Place" through "his own blood, thus securing an eternal redemption." Through his blood shed on the cross he *"offered himself without blemish to God"* through the "eternal Spirit" (cf. Heb 9:11–14).
> *The one Priesthood of Christ is eternal and definitive,* just as the sacrifice he offered is definitive and eternal. Every day and always, especially during the Sacred Triduum, this truth lives in the Church's consciousness: "We have a great high priest" (Heb 4:14).[6]

This text of John Paul II takes quotes from the Letter to the Hebrews that refer to the priestly category of the Old Testament. The priesthood of the old covenant, mediation between men and God, was characterized by three elements: the priests were instituted (1) according to precise conditions, (2) to offer sensible sacrifices, and (3) to obtain the forgiveness of God. In fact, the high priests, who came exclusively from priestly families (this was a necessary condition), were charged with preparing themselves annually to enter the sanctuary and offer sacrifices in expiation for their sins and those of the people of Israel. These repetitive rites, which were ineffective in perfectly achieving the end pursued (the forgiveness of God), were

---

5 *Letter* 1987, no. 3. At a general audience, the pope says: "It is indeed good that everyone should know the Church's doctrine on the priesthood and what she desires of those who, having received it, are conformed to the sublime image of Christ, the eternal Priest and most pure Victim of the salvific sacrifice. That image is developed in the *Letter to the Hebrews* and in other texts of the Apostles and Evangelists, and has been handed on faithfully in the Church's tradition of thought and life. Today too it is necessary for the clergy to be faithful to that image, which mirrors the living truth of Christ the Priest and Victim" (*General Audience*, June 9, 1993, no. 1).

6 *Letter* 1989, no. 1, emphasis in the original.

the foreshadowing of a better and perfect sacrifice, that of Christ: his "one Priesthood [. . .] is eternal and definitive, just as the sacrifice he offered is definitive and eternal." The priesthood of Christ is unique and essentially united to his own sacrifice.

A New Condition

John Paul II, above all, recalls the novelty and superiority of the priesthood of Christ. These expressions particularly demonstrate his thought.

> When [. . .] we pray: *Iesu, Sacerdos in aeternum secundum ordinem Melchisedech*, our thoughts go back to the Old Testament, to Psalm 110. We all know what it means that Christ is a priest like Melchisedech. His priesthood was expressed in the offering of his own body, "once for all" (Heb 10:10). He who offered himself as a bloody sacrifice on the Cross also instituted its unbloody "memorial" for all times, under the species of bread and wine. And under these species he entrusted his Sacrifice to the Church. In this way the Church—and in the Church every priest—celebrates the one Sacrifice of Christ.[7]

The quote from Psalm 110 (109) refers to the mysterious figure of Melchizedech.[8] He is a prefiguration of Christ: he is of a different priestly category and is superior to what hitherto existed. Indeed, Jesus did not come from a priestly family, and He is not confined by the conditions required by the tradition of Israel. Besides, his priesthood is eternal because the mediation of Christ has an incomparable extension. This, then, is what the novelty and superiority of the priesthood of Christ is: "He was not, indeed, simply welcomed for a moment by God and then sent back to the people, as the high priest who penetrated a few moments in the holy of holies. He has been welcomed definitively and now participates, in his glorified

---

7 *Letter* 1997, no. 3. Cf. also *Letter* 1985, no. 1: "[H]e is also the ineffable *victim* of his own Priesthood in the sacrifice of Golgotha. During the Last Supper, he left to the Church this sacrifice of his—the sacrifice of the new and eternal Covenant—as the *Eucharist*: the sacrament of his body and blood under the appearances of bread and wine 'after the order of Melchizedech' (Ps 110[109], 4; cf. Heb 7:17)." Emphasis in the original.

8 "Without father, mother, or ancestry, without beginning of days or end of life, thus made to resemble the Son of God, he remains a priest forever" (Heb 7:3). Cf. commentary by Albert Vanhoye, *La lettre aux hébreux* (Paris: Desclée, 2002), 115–24. He summarizes, on page 123: "The membership of the tribe of Levi was a condition for the levitical priesthood. One thus becomes a priest 'according to a law of carnal prescription' (Heb 7:16a) and, consequently, for the limited time of a carnal existence. Christ, on the contrary, is a priest because of his victory over death,

humanity, with divine eternity,"[9] and He intercedes forever in our favor at the right hand of the Father.[10]

His work is all the more effective and real because He has all the qualities required to fulfill it. Only He is truly capable of doing this. Indeed, He is God and perfect man, Son of God and brother of men, merciful by His spotless humanity, who has learned suffering and is "worthy of faith" from the Father through His divinity. This makes Him supportive of men. He is thus able to help us effectively (Heb 4:16) because "He has all the divine authority and all the human sensibility."[11] The pope says:

> During the Sacred Triduum, the one *priesthood* of the new and everlasting Covenant is made visible to the eyes of our faith, the priesthood *which is in Christ himself*. To him indeed can be applied the words *about the high priest* who, "*chosen from among* men, is appointed to act on their behalf" (cf. Heb 5:1). *As man Christ is Priest*; he is "high priest of the good things that have come." At the same time, however, this man-priest is the Son, of one being with the Father. For this reason his priesthood—the priesthood of his redemptive sacrifice—is one and unrepeatable.[12]

A New Sacrifice

Concerning the second element necessary for the priesthood, John Paul II affirms that "the sacrifice of the 'new and everlasting' covenant [. . .] is intimately connected with the mystery of the Incarnation: the Word who became flesh (cf. Jn 1:14) immolates his humanity as *homo assumptus* in the unity of the divine Person."[13] Thus, at Easter, "the Son of God, as Redeemer of the world, will fulfill the Father's will through the offering and the immolation of his Body and Blood on Golgotha."[14]

---

so that his priesthood will no longer meet any limit. This victory is due to 'an indestructible power of life' (Heb 7:16). [. . .] So there is a change of priesthood. A perfect and definitive mediation has replaced a defective and temporary mediation."

9 Vanhoye, *La lettre aux hébreux*, 118.

10 Cf. Penitential Act 6: "You are seated at the right hand of the Father to intercede for us: Lord, have mercy." *The Roman Missal* (New Jersey: Catholic Book Publishing, 2011).

11 Vanhoye, *La lettre aux hébreux*, 84.

12 *Letter* 1989, no. 3, emphasis in the original.

13 *Letter* 1988, no. 1.

14 *Letter* 1988, no. 1.

By this sacrifice, He abolishes all other sacrifices to become the only perfect mediator between God and men.[15] Indeed, in the old covenant, the offerings presented to God were made by imperfect mediators: the priests themselves had to make sacrifices every year for the atonement of their own sins and for those of the people. In Jesus, we have a "high priest" who "entered once for all into the sanctuary [. . .] with his own blood" for He is truly accredited by the Father.[16] He is sinless and perfect,[17] both as a priest and as a victim: for this reason He offers Himself only once. "Christ is priest of his own sacrifice," and his mediation gets us a result that is always effective.[18]

A Perfectly Accomplished Goal

Regarding the third element that I initially mentioned—the goal of the priestly offering—no other sacrifice could achieve a better result: the "eternal redemption," the "of the good things that have come." Through the paschal mystery of Christ and through his priestly mediation, the whole of humanity is now invited to walk with confidence on the path that leads to salvation and reorients it to its original destiny.

> The redemption is accomplished through the sacrifice in which Christ—the Mediator of the new and eternal covenant—"entered once for all into the Holy Place with his own blood," making room in the "house of the Father"—in the bosom of the Most Holy Trinity—for all "those who are called to the eternal inheritance" (cf. Heb 9:12, 15). It is precisely for this reason that the crucified and risen Christ is "the high

---

15 "Christ, the Priest and Victim, is as such, the artisan of universal salvation, in obedience to the Father. He is the one High Priest of the new and eternal Covenant, who by accomplishing our salvation offers perfect worship to the Father, a worship which ancient celebrations of the Old Testament merely prefigured. By the sacrifice of his own blood on the cross, Christ 'entered once for all into the sanctuary. . ., thus obtaining eternal redemption' (Heb 9:12). Thus he abolished every ancient sacrifice in order to establish a new one by offering himself to Father's will (Ps 40 [39], 9). 'By this will, we have been consecrated through the offering of the body of Jesus Christ once for all. . . . For by one offering he has made perfect forever those who are being consecrated (Heb 10:10–14)" (*General Audience*, May 12, 1993, no. 1).

16 "Faithful high priest before God" (Heb 2:17), that is to say, he has authority for dealing with God. Cf. Vanhoye, *La lettre aux hébreux*, 70–81.

17 "'Our high priest has been tested in all our likeness, except sin' (Heb 4:15). [. . .] Holiness and moral integrity fulfill, indeed, an essential role for the glorification of Christ and for his mediation." Vanhoye, *La lettre aux hébreux*, 132.s

18 "Christ is the priest of his own sacrifice: 'Through the eternal spirit he offered himself without blemish to God' (Heb 9:14)" (*Letter* 1996, no. 1).

priest of the good things to come" (Heb 9:11) and his sacrifice means a new orientation of man's spiritual history towards God, the Creator and Father, towards whom the first-born of all creation leads all in the Holy Spirit.[19]

It can be perceived that the three elements of the old priesthood are taken up and brought to perfection by Christ.

To conclude this section, I can say that the pope affirms that the priesthood in Christ is more than a function: priesthood belongs to the identity of Christ. This is not because He submitted to particular rites (cf. Ex 20, Lv 8), but because, in His priestly role as mediator, He is the only one capable, by His being, to truly connect with one another, His brothers, with whom He is perfectly assimilated by nature, and God, with whom He shares divine nature: Jesus "had to become like his brothers in every way, that he might be a merciful and faithful high priest before God" (Heb 2:17).[20] He has definitely replaced all other mediators and sacrifices by His eternal and perfect adherence to the Father's will to save men and by the offering of His sacrifice, which was made possible by His Incarnation (cf. Heb 2:17).[21]

> This is an objective reality: by assuming a human nature in the Incarnation, the eternal Son of God fulfilled the necessary condition for becoming the one Priest of humanity through his death and resurrection (cf. Heb 5:1). [. . .] The Letter to the Hebrews reveals that when he "came into the world," Jesus gave a priestly orientation towards his personal sacrifice and

---

19 *Letter* 1988, no. 7. Dash after "towards God" is changed to a comma to make better sense of the passage.

20 Translation of Vanhoye, *La lettre aux hébreux*, 15.

21 "The mystery of the priesthood has its beginning in the Trinity and is, at the same time, a consequence of the Incarnation" (*Letter* 1996, no. 1). Also, the "author of the Letter to the Hebrews emphasizes that Christ's priesthood is linked to the sacrifice of the Cross: 'Christ appeared as a high priest of the good things to come, then through the greater and more perfect tabernacle (not made with hands, that is, not of this creation), he entered once for all into the Holy Place, taking his own blood, thus securing an eternal redemption' (Heb 9:11–12)" (*Letter* 1996, no. 1). Similarly, in his *Letter* 2000, no. 7, he writes: "The Jubilee invites us to contemplate the intimate link between Christ's priesthood and the mystery of his person. The priesthood of Christ is not 'incidental,' a task which he might or might not have assumed: rather, it is integral to his identity as the Son Incarnate, as God-made-man." And also: "The Church invokes the Holy Spirit as *spiritalis unctio*, anointing of the soul. Through the anointing of the Spirit in the immaculate womb of Mary, the Father consecrated Christ the Eternal High Priest of the New Covenant who wished to share his priesthood with us, calling us to be his presence in history for the salvation of our brothers and sisters" (*Letter* 1998, no. 2).

said to God: "Sacrifice and offering you did not desire, but a body you prepared for me [. . .] then I said, behold, I come [. . .] to do your will, O God"
(Heb 10:5, 7).[22]

Vocation and Service

The Priestly Ministry is a Vocation . . .

The pope emphasizes on several occasions that the priestly ministry is a
vocation, and in the image of the call of Christ.

Christ [. . .] too was called to the priesthood. It is the Father who
"calls" his own Son, whom he has begotten by an act of eternal
love, to "come into the world" (cf. Heb 10:5) and to become man.
He wills that his only-begotten Son, by taking flesh, should
become "a priest forever": the one priest of the new eternal Covenant. The Son's vocation to the priesthood expresses the depth
of the Trinitarian mystery. For only the Son, the Word of the
Father, in whom and through whom all things were created, can
unceasingly offer creation in sacrifice to the Father, confirming
that everything created has come forth from the Father and must
become an offering of praise to the Creator. Thus the mystery of
the priesthood has its beginning in the Trinity and is, at the same
time, a consequence of the Incarnation. By becoming man, the
only-begotten and eternal Son of the Father is born of woman,
enters into the created order and thus becomes a priest, the one
eternal priest. [. . .] The priesthood of Christ is rooted in the work
of redemption.[23]

It can simply be said that the priesthood is "gift and mystery."[24] "Gift"
because, ultimately, it is a call and a free initiative of God; "mystery" because
it is fundamentally rooted in the heart of the Trinity and leads to its communion of love.[25]

---

22 *General Audience*, June 30, 1993, no. 2.

23 *Letter* 1996, no. 1. The mystery of the Incarnation, to which the pope often returns, seems to
us to be understood as the mystery of the whole life of Jesus, that is to say, "the work of redemption," which includes passion, death, resurrection, ascension into heaven, and the gift of the
Holy Spirit.

24 Cf. the title of John Paul II's homonymous book: *Gift and Mystery: On the Fiftieth Anniversary
of My Priestly Ordination* (New York: Image Books, 1996).

25 This subject will be dealt with in the third chapter of this work, when I speak of the mission
of the priestly ministry.

The gift of being a priest is an "honor" that cannot be arrogated. Like Christ, one is "appointed" priest by God.[26] It is not achieved by ambition to acquire a position, to be above the others. One can only receive the priesthood humbly because one does not claim glory in becoming a priest (Heb 5:5).

> The priesthood is a call, a particular vocation: "one does not take this honour upon himself, but he is called by God" (Heb 5:4). The Letter to the Hebrews harks back to the priesthood of the Old Testament in order to lead us to an understanding of the mystery of Christ the Priest: "Christ did not exalt himself to be made a high priest, but was appointed by him who said to him: . . . You are a priest for ever, after the order of Melchizedek" (Heb 5:5–6).[27]

Having been called, Jesus responds generously to the Father's call to do His will and to fulfill the mission He has entrusted to Him.

> The Letter to the Hebrews [places] on the lips of Christ the words of Psalm 40: "You desired neither sacrifice nor offering, but instead you prepared a body for me. . . . Here I am . . . I come to do your will, O God" (Heb 10:5–7; cf. Ps 40:7–9). According to the author of the Letter, these prophetic words were spoken by Christ when he first came into the world. They express his mystery and his mission. They begin to be accomplished from the very moment of the Incarnation and reach their completion in the sacrifice of Golgotha. From that time forward, every priestly offering is but a re-presenting to the Father of the one offering of Christ, made once for all.[28]

---

26 "One does not take for oneself honour, but one is appointed by God" (Heb 5:4). Translation of Vanhoye, *La lettre aux hébreux*, 94. But unlike Christ, the ordained minister knows that he is not immaculate like Him (Heb 4:15). It is for this reason that John Paul II recalls the importance of the sacrament of Reconciliation in the life of the priest: "Does not the *Letter to the Hebrews* say of the priest, taken from among men: 'He is able to deal patiently with the ignorant and erring, for he himself is beset by weakness' (Heb 5:2)? [. . .] The personal use of the sacrament of Penance motivates the priest to make himself more available to administering this sacrament to the faithful who request it" (*General Audience*, June 2, 1993, no. 6).

27 *Letter* 1996, Introduction.

28 *Letter* 2000, no. 8. The verses of the Letter to the Hebrews quoted in this passage are also an occasion for the Holy Father to manifest his Marian piety: "*Christ the Priest* [. . .] addresses his Eternal Father in these words: 'Sacrifices and offerings you have not desired, but a body you have prepared for me. In burnt offerings and sin offerings you have taken no pleasure. Then I said, "Lo, I have come to do your will, O God" (Heb 10:5–7). *These words in some way also involve his Mother*, since the Eternal Father formed Christ's body by the power of the Holy Spirit in the womb of the Virgin Mary, thanks also to her consent: 'Let it be to me according to your word' (Lk 1:38)" (*Letter* 1995, no. 1, emphasis in the original).

Therefore, it can be affirmed with the Pope that "the priesthood of the New Covenant, to which we are called in the Church, is therefore a share in this unique priesthood of Christ."[29] The priesthood is an election and a response to this call. It follows that in the exercise of the priestly ministry, "the whole mystery of the Incarnation must be alive in our minds and hearts. Christ, who on Holy Thursday announces that his body will be 'given up' and his blood 'shed,' is the eternal Son, who 'coming into the world,' says to the Father: 'A body you prepared for me [. . .], I come to do your will' (cf. Heb 10:5–7)."[30]

. . . and a Mission

To speak of the "will of the Father" is to deal with the question of the mission of the Son, as I have mentioned, because the priesthood is a gift for service (Heb 5:1). It is also the meaning of the mission of one who is *alter Christus*—another Christ:[31] "The priest, who, having been 'chosen from among men,' is appointed to act *on behalf of men in relation to God*' (Heb 5:1). The human dimension of priestly service, in order to be fully authentic, must be rooted in God. Indeed, in every way that this service is 'on behalf of men,' it is also 'in relation to God.'"[32]

Essentially, this relationship with God is established—according to John Paul II—by the conduct of men towards salvation, by the proclamation of the Gospel and the administration of the sacraments, especially the Eucharist. Ultimately, the priestly missions are to teach, to sanctify, and to govern.

---

29 *Letter* 1996, no. 1. Here again one perceives a novelty: Christ wanted to share his priesthood with others, in a kind of integration. This is very far from the priestly category of the Old Testament, characterized by separation at different levels (the family origin, the place of the offering, the contact with the rest of the people . . .).

30 *Letter* 1988, no. 1.

31 Cf. *Letter* 1991, no. 2. "As a result the priest has a sort of mastery of grace, which allows him to enjoy union with Christ and at the same time to be devoted to the pastoral service of his brothers and sisters" (*General Audience*, May 26, 1993, no. 2). The third chapter of this work will deal more extensively with the theme of the priest's mission.

32 *Letter* 1991, no. 2, emphasis in the original. This rooting in Christ is typological for the priest: "The priest thus finds in Christ the model of a true love for the suffering, the poor, the afflicted and especially for sinners, because Jesus is close to human beings with a life like our own; he endured trials and tribulations like our own, therefore he is full of compassion for us and 'is able to deal patiently with erring sinners' (Heb 5:2). Finally, he is able effectively to help those sorely tried 'Since he was himself tested through what he suffered, he is able to help those who are tempted' (Heb 2:18)" (*General Audience*, July 7, 1993, no. 4).

Over and above our commitment to the evangelical mission, our greatest commitment consists in exercising this mysterious power over the body of the Redeemer, and all that is within us should be decisively ordered to this. We should also always remember that to this ministerial power we have been sacramentally consecrated, that we have been chosen from among men "for the good of men" (Heb 5:1). We especially, the priests of the Latin Church, whose ordination rite added in the course of the centuries the custom of anointing the priest's hands, should think about this.[33]

Finally, "[a]ll that Christ did and taught was at the service of our redemption. The ultimate and most complete expression of this messianic service was to be the *Cross on Calvary*. The Cross confirmed in the fullest possible way that the Son of God became man 'for us men and for our salvation' (creed of the Mass). And this *salvific service*, which embraces the whole universe, is 'inscribed' forever in the Priesthood of Christ."[34] It is for this reason that, in "an effort to correspond fully to that 'anointing with the Spirit of the Lord,' which establishes him in the ministerial priesthood, the priest cannot fulfill the expectations that people—the Church and the world—rightly place in him."[35]

"Priest for Eternity"

We come to the third and final aspect of John Paul II's reading of the Letter to the Hebrews. Having affirmed the uniqueness and the novelty of the priesthood of Christ, recalling that the participation in his priesthood is a call and a service, the Holy Father goes on to conclude that the priestly mediation of the Son is always at work in the world.

---

33 *Letter* 1980, no. 11.

34 *Letter* 1989, no. 4, emphasis in the original. The ordained ministry is closely united to Christ and "[t]his concern *shows* in the best possible way *who the priest is for the laity*. It testifies to his identity, [. . .] for the priesthood is a 'social' sacrament" (*Letter* 1989, no. 4). And also: "This mark [the indelible character], impressed in the depths of our being, has its 'personalistic' dynamism. *The priestly personality must be for others* a clear and plain *sign and indication*. This is the first condition for our pastoral service. The people from among whom we have been chosen and for whom we have been appointed want above all to see in us such a sign and indication" (*Letter* 1979, no. 7, emphasis in the original). Henceforth the priesthood of the new covenant has "a positive efficacy to unite God deeply to the human person" (Vanhoye, *La lettre aux hébreux*, 26).

35 *Letter* 1991, no. 2. The "priest is bound to a special imitation of Christ the Priest, which is the result of the special grace of Orders: the grace of union with Christ the Priest and Victim, by virtue of this same union, the grace of *good pastoral service to his brothers and sisters*" (*General Audience*, May 26, 1993, no. 2, emphasis in the original).

From now on, the relationship between mankind and God passes wholly through Christ: "No one comes to the Father, except through me" (Jn 14:6). This is why Christ is a priest endowed with an eternal and universal priesthood, of which the priesthood of the first Covenant was a prefigurement and a preparation. He has exercised it fully from the moment he took his seat as High Priest "at the right hand of the throne of the Majesty in heaven" (Heb 8:1). From that time forth, the very nature of human priesthood changed: now there is but one priesthood, that of Christ, which can be shared and exercised in different ways.[36]

Among these different ways of participating in the priesthood of Christ[37] and its actualization, that of the ordained ministers is specific.

[T]he priesthood, in every degree, and thus, in both bishops and presbyters, is a participation in the priesthood of Christ, who, according to the *Letter to the Hebrews*, is the "High Priest" of the new and eternal Covenant, who "offered himself once for all" in a sacrifice of infinite value that remains unchangeable and unceasing at the very heart of the economy of salvation (cf. Heb 7:24–28). There is no further need or possibility of other priests in addition to or alongside the one mediator, Christ (cf. Heb 9:15; Rm 5:15–19; 1 Tm 2:5), the point of union and reconciliation between mankind and God (cf. 2 Cor 5:14–20), the Word made flesh, full of grace (cf. Jn 1:1–18), the true and definitive *hiereus*, Priest (cf. Heb 5:6; 10:21) who on earth "took away sin by his sacrifice" (Heb 9:26) and in heaven continues to make intercession for his faithful (cf. Heb 7:25), until they attain the heavenly inheritance won and promised by him. No one else in the new Covenant is *hiereus* in the same sense.[38]

---

36 *Letter* 2000, no. 7. Since the sacrifice of Christ is self-sufficient and effective today, it has been offered "once for all" (Heb 9:12) because "a unique and effective personal offering has replaced the external offerings, indefinitely repeated and inefficient" (Vanhoye, *La lettre aux hébreux*, 149). A transformation of the priesthood took place. On the other hand, the session at the right hand of God is not static but active, because his intercession is permanent (cf. Vanhoye, *La lettre aux hébreux*, 138).

37 The first mode of ontological participation in the priesthood of Christ is established by Baptism. Through him we become "priests" (1 Pt 2:10), and "the fundamental duty" of the "'universal priesthood' is to worship God" (*General Audience*, March 25, 1992, no. 6). Ordained ministers receive "a *special consecration*, in relationship to Baptism and Confirmation; a *deeper configuration to Christ the Priest*, who makes them his active ministers in the official worship of God" (*General Audience*, March 31, 1993, no. 6, emphasis in the original). The cultic element is common to all: Christ offers himself to the Father for men, the faithful offer the worship of their life to God, the priests offer themselves and offer the sacrifice of Christ.

38 *General Audience*, March 31, 1993, no. 2.

The "mystery of the redemption of the world" is realized in today's history thanks to the "ministers of the sacrifice."[39] The glorification of Christ in heaven did not put an end to his priestly mediation for men, for he "is the same yesterday, today, and forever" (Heb 13:8)[40]:

> As we repeat these invocations [of the Litany of Jesus Christ, Priest and Victim], we see with the eyes of faith what is spoken of by the Letter to the Hebrews. As a Priest eternally consecrated by the Father in *Spiritu Sancto et virtute*, Jesus now "is seated at the right hand of the Majesty on high" (Heb 1:3). And from there he intercedes for us as our Mediator—*semper vivens ad interpellandum pro nobis*—in order to blaze for us the path of a new, eternal life: *Pontifex qui nobis viam novam initiasti*. He loves us, and he shed his blood in order to wash away our sins—*Pontifex qui dilexisti nos et lavasti nos a peccatis in sanguine tuo*. He gave himself for us: *tradidisti temetipsum Deo oblationem et hostiam*.[41]

Rather, the glorified state of Jesus has strengthened His mediation[42] since "Christ has entered an eternal sanctuary, 'into heaven itself, now to appear in the presence of God on our behalf' (Heb 9:24)."[43] This manifests

---

39 *Letter* 1993, no. 1. Indeed, "we have *received* this ineffable gift *so that we may be ministers* of Christ's *going forth* by way of the cross and, at the same time, of his *coming* in the Eucharist. [. . .] We are ministers of the mystery of the redemption of the world, ministers of the Body which was offered and of the Blood which was shed so that sins might be forgiven. Ministers of that Sacrifice by which he, alone, entered once for all into the Holy Place. 'Having offered himself without blemish to God, he purifies our conscience from dead works to serve the living God' (Heb 9:14)" (*Letter* 1993, no. 1). Cf. also *Letter* 1990, no. 1: "It was on that day that each of us saw himself, in the Priesthood of Christ in the Upper Room, as a minister of the Eucharist [. . .]. It was on this day that each of us, by virtue of the sacrament, saw this Priesthood as accomplished in himself, as imprinted on his soul in the form of an indelible seal: 'You are a priest forever (Heb 5:6).'"

40 Vanhoye, *La lettre aux hébreux*, 81: "The author [of the Letter to the Hebrews] does not specify [. . .] that this authority comes to them from participation in the priestly authority of the glorified Christ, but there is little risk of being mistaken in attributing to him this thought, for immediately after saying, 'Remember your leaders, who have told you the word of God; consider how their life ended and imitate their faith' (Heb 13:7), he declares: 'Jesus Christ is the same yesterday and today, and for the ages' (Heb 13:8). [. . .] Christ [. . .] makes present his priestly mediation by the ministry of the leaders of his Church."

41 *Letter* 1997, no. 4.

42 Indeed, according to Vanhoye, *La lettre aux hébreux*, 147: "The writer [of the Letter to the Hebrews] went beyond appearances, and he acknowledged that this event had fully accomplished what the ancient rites tried in vain to achieve and could only figure, the entrance from the high priest to the true sanctuary, that is to say the elevation of the human nature of Christ into the heavenly intimacy of God (Heb 9:24)."

43 *Letter* 1989, no. 4. Being in heaven He reveals to us our heavenly calling (Heb 3:1) and invites us to enter into God's rest (Heb 3:7–4:11).

concretely in the world, where He continues His "service,"[44] since the sacraments and especially the Eucharist

> are the continual presence and action of Christ, "the Holy One" of God (Lk 1:34; Jn 6:69; Acts 3:14; Rev 3:7), "anointed with the Holy Spirit" (Acts 10:38; Lk 4:18), "consecrated by the Father" (Jn 10:36) to lay down His life of His own accord and to take it up again (Cf. Jn 10:17), and the High Priest of the New Covenant (Heb 3:1; 4:15). For it is He who, represented by the celebrant, makes His entrance into the sanctuary and proclaims His Gospel. It is He who is "the offerer and the offered, the consecrator and the consecrated" (Barberini Greco 366 f. 8 verso, lines 17–20).[45]

Consequently, when "we renew the Passover of Christ, 'his hour' (cf. Jn 2:4; 13:1), which is the blessed 'fullness of time' (cf. Gal 4:4),"[46] the ordained minister actualizes the action of Christ in our time.[47] The priest is thus conscious of being forever configured to Him, by virtue of the sacrament of Holy Orders. He can now count on the grace of Christ and renew unceasingly his fidelity in Him who supports him because he is united in a particular way to Christ. Christ is "the eternal and unceasing source of our priesthood in the Church."[48]

> On this day [Holy Thursday] *every year we renew the promises we made* in connection with the Sacrament of the Priesthood. These promises have great implications. What is at stake is the word we have given to Christ himself. *Fidelity to our vocation builds up the Church,* and every act of infidelity is a painful wound to the Mystical Body of Christ. And so, as we gather together and contemplate the mystery of the institution of the

---

44 *Letter* 1989, no. 4: "Christ, who came to serve, is *sacramentally present in the Eucharist*[—sacrament of Christ's redeeming sacrifice—]precisely in order to serve. At the same time this service is the fullness of salvific mediation."

45 *Letter* 1980, no. 8.

46 *Letter* 1993, no. 1.

47 Similarly, the pope writes, "In speaking of the priests' prayer, the Council also mentions and recommends the Liturgy of the Hours, which joins the priest's personal prayer to that of the Church. 'In reciting the Divine Office,' it says, 'they lend their voice to the Church which perseveres in prayer in the name of the whole human race, in union with Christ who always lives to make intercession for them (Heb 7:25)' (PO 13)" (*General Audience,* June 2, 1993, no. 5).

48 *Letter* 1985, no. 1.

Eucharist and the Priesthood, let us implore our High Priest who, as Sacred Scripture says, showed himself to be faithful (cf. Heb 2:17), that we too may remain faithful. In the spirit of this "sacramental brotherhood" let us pray for one another—priests for priests! May Holy Thursday become for us a renewed call to cooperate with the grace of the Sacrament of the Priesthood![49]

Synthesis

The scriptural reference given by John Paul II is a fundamental point of reference for his reflection on the priesthood.

By frequently using the Letter to the Hebrews, the Holy Father recognizes in Christ his priestly function. Indeed, this epistle is the only text of the New Testament that explicitly uses the word "priest" with respect to Christ.[50] But this priesthood of Christ is fundamentally new: it now excludes belonging to a race. It is no longer an external worship but an internal one, because it is his own flesh that is offered and not that of animals. It is unique in its effect and it does not repeat itself. There is therefore a continuity with what characterizes the elements of the old priesthood, but it is qualitatively new in its content.[51]

Also, when Christ engages others in his priesthood, He calls them for a service. He chooses them from among those whom He wants (cf. Mk 3:13). He transforms the interior of their being to make them capable of offering His sacrifice,[52] the effectiveness of which is always present by His sacramental representation.[53] Thus, the priesthood of Christ

---

49 *Letter* 1994, no. 4, emphasis in the original.

50 However, the New Testament uses, with parsimony, a priestly terminology, either relative to Christ or to the ecclesial ministry. This prudence could perhaps be explained by a desire of the apostolic community to distance itself from Judaism and its worship. Cf. Gisbert Greshake, *Essere preti in questo tempo* (Brescia: Queriniana, 2008), 94.

51 Jesus Himself had announced a new priesthood: "Destroy this temple and in three days I will raise it up" (Jn 2:19). By the resurrection of Christ the temple is rebuilt by the power of God. In the sacrifice of the Lord and in His resurrection, the priestly heritage of the Old Alliance is perpetuated. It finds its completion and is transformed into a new priesthood (cf. speech of Cardinal Joseph Ratzinger, at the anniversary of the Decree *Presbyterorum Ordinis*, October 23–28, 1995, available at http://www.clerus.org/clerus/dati/1998–12/13–6/Ratzinger_symposio.rtf.html).

52 This transformation of the interior of being announces the notion of "character," which will be discussed in chapter 2.

53 Chapter 3—The Priest, "Memory" of Christ—will invoke the strength of the sacramental reality that governs the life and action of the priest. He "makes present" in the Church and in the world the work of salvation of Christ.

entrusted to the Church no longer consists of simply being designated to celebrate rites. The priesthood of Christ transforms the real existence of the one who receives the ordained ministry[54] through the action of the Holy Spirit.

In the letters to Priests that have been discussed, it is ascertained that in using the Epistle to the Hebrews, John Paul II is fundamentally interpreting the priesthood of Christ in light of the mystery of his Incarnation. He thus joins the spirituality of the *École Française*.[55] However, the pope goes further—perhaps discreetly—by reflecting more faithfully the thought of the author of the Epistle to the Hebrews, for whom the priestly consecration of the Lord is the whole of the work of the Redemption, which in itself includes the mystery of the whole life of the Savior.[56]

Finally, the scriptural reference to Christ is paramount and had to be presented at the very beginning of this journey. This reference will require

---

54 Those who receive Baptism become members of the priestly people (cf. Ex 19:6; Rev 5:10) and are also transformed internally. This will be briefly discussed in chapter 2.

55 Priestly formation in Polish lands was marked by this spirituality thanks to the presence of Vincentians, who arrived in September 1651, to whom the priestly formation was entrusted (among others in Krakow since 1770). Also, according to some (as reported in my personal exchanges with Cardinal Georges-Marie Cottier, Laurent Touze, or Jan Duka, CM), John Paul II integrated the model of priests trained by this congregation, as well as by the readings conveyed to his time.

Pierre de Bérulle (1575–1629), founder of the *Oratoire*, is one of the great figures of the *École Française*. He sees priestly spirituality as a spirituality closely related to the mystery of the Incarnation. In fact, the Word of God assumes the humanity of the priest and makes the priestly state the origin of the holiness that exists in the Church: each priest is a manifestation of Christ Himself, hence his very high dignity.

Also, the ordained ministry was perceived primarily as a means of personal sanctification, as was the profession of vows for religious. Cf. Michel Dupuy, *Bérulle et le sacerdoce. Étude historique et doctrinale. Textes inédits* (Paris: Lethielleux, 1969), 410. This elevated vision of the priest, which distinguished him and separated him from others and required a consistent life of union with God, was shared by Charles de Condren, Jean-Jacques Olier, and Jean Eudes. This perspective has led to a gradual distance between priests and laypeople.

Saint Vincent de Paul finds a greater balance between the exaltation of the priesthood and the pastoral service. Cf. Luigi Mezzadri, *A lode e gloria. Il sacerdozio nell'École Française* (Milan: Jaca Book, 1989), 9–32. Here, one realizes more that the teaching of John Paul II joined this development of the *École Française*: the priest is the man chosen by God for the service of men. This will be seen in the course of this book.

56 I evoke here *Letter* 1996, no. 1, and I recall his affirmation that "the priesthood of Christ is rooted in the work of redemption." The Paschal mystery—passion and glorification—will be for Christ the implementation of his "priestly being," of his "priestly consecration"—that is to say, the fundamental moment by which He makes man capable to restore without barriers a relationship of filial union with God. Also, the "eternal Spirit" (Heb 9:14), Spirit of Fire (cf. Acts 2:3; Lv 8:21), consecrates his offering by introducing it into glory (cf. Vanhoye, *La lettre aux hébreux*, 15–29).

placing the priestly ministry in the mystery of the Church (chapter 2) and in her mission (chapter 3). From this foundation, one grasps the coherence of the pope's thought on the priesthood: ontologically participating in the unique priesthood of Christ, the ordained minister is called to serve the baptized and to reorient humanity towards God, thus specifically collaborating with the work of salvation.

THE TRADITION

In this part of the book, as well as in the following section, it is necessary to analyze some sources drawn on by John Paul II in Tradition and in the Magisterium, mentioned in his *Letters*. Although they are much less numerous than the scriptural sources, they are no less interesting.

In the *Letters* of John Paul II there are seventeen references to ecclesiastical authors:[57] Ignatius of Antioch (35–113),[58] Irenaeus of Lyon (130–202),[59] Hippolytus of Rome (170–235),[60] Cyprian (200–258),[61] Gregory of Nazianzus (329–390),[62] Augustine (354–430),[63] Gregory the Great (540–604),[64] and Thomas Aquinas (1225–1274).[65]

In studying these quotations, three main ideas emerge: above all, the theme of unity, then the action of the Holy Spirit, and finally the question of the pastoral dimension of the ministerial priesthood.[66] I propose to present these themes and the use of the authors mentioned.

---

57 By "ecclesiastical authors" I am referring to the Fathers of the Church as well as other theologians or ancient doctors.

58 *Epistula ad Magnesios*, VI,1, in the *Letter* 1979, no. 1.

59 *Adversus hæreses* III,17,3 and 24,1, in the *Letter* 1998, no. 3 and no. 6. Also *Adversus hæreses* IV,20,7, in *Letter* 1996, no. 6.

60 The *Apostolic Tradition* of Saint Hippolytus, nos. 2–4, in the *Letter* 1980, no. 2.

61 *The Lord's Prayer*, 23, in *Letter* 2000, no. 5.

62 *Theological Poems*, I,1,1,2, in *Letter* 1998, no. 6.

63 Augustine is quoted six times: *Sermon* 340,1 (three times: *Letters* 1979, no. 1, 1985, no. 2, and 2001, no. 10); *In Evangelium Ioannis*, 31,13 (*Letter* 1980, no. 5) and 26,13 (*Letter* 1980, Conclusion); and *Confessions* III,VI,11 (*Letter* 1985, no. 5).

64 *Regula Pastoralis* 1,1 (*Letter* 1979, no. 6) and *Homilies on Ezekiel*, II,7,7 (*Letter* 1998, no. 3).

65 *Summa Theologiae* I-II, q. 68, a. 2 (*Letter* 1998, no. 4), and *Contra Gentiles*, IV, 22 (*Letter* 1998, no. 4).

66 I will return to this topic in chapter 3.

Signum unitatis—Sign of Unity

When John Paul II quotes the Fathers of the Church, the first theme that emerges is that of unity or communion.[67] It comes in different aspects: Eucharistic unity, ecclesial unity, and hierarchical unity.

The priesthood is fundamentally united to the Eucharist. The accounts of the institution of the Eucharist attest to this,[68] of course, as do the oldest writings: "Through our ordination—the celebration of which is linked to the holy Mass from the very first liturgical evidence (cf. *Apostolic Tradition* of Saint Hippolytus, 2–4)—we are united in a singular and exceptional way to the Eucharist."[69]

What has been said in the previous paragraphs could be perceived as a little too "individualistic," too self-centered between the priest and the Eucharist. In reality, in this relationship between the priesthood and the Eucharist, the pope wishes to underline and highlight the link between the priest and communion in the Church, for "the doctrine of the Eucharist" as "sign of unity and bond of charity" was "taught by Saint Paul, (1 Cor 10:17, commented on by Saint Augustine, *In Evangelium Ioannis* 31,13, and by the Ecumenical Council of Trent, sess. XII, chap. 8) has been in subsequent times deepened by the writings of very many saints."[70] Still relying on Augustine, John Paul II makes an appeal marked by the pain of divisions but, at the same time, filled with confident hope.

> Above all I wish to emphasize that the problems of the liturgy, and in particular of the Eucharistic Liturgy, must not be an occasion of dividing Catholics and for threatening the unity of the Church. This is demanded by an elementary understanding of that sacrament which Christ has left us as the source of spiritual unity. And how could the Eucharist, which in

---

67 The phrase *signum unitatis* that titles this section comes from Augustine, *In Evangelium Ioannis*, 26,13, quoted in *Letter* 1980, conclusion.

68 This subject will be discussed further in the second chapter of this work.

69 *Letter* 1980, no. 2. Indeed, the prayer of episcopal consecration asks God that the newly elected "offers the gifts of your holy Church" (*Apostolic Tradition*, no. 3). Then, "as soon as he is consecrated, the new bishop will exercise his priesthood by celebrating the Eucharist with the presbyterium. The deacon brings the gifts and immediately the bishop imposes his hands with the priests. By imitating the gesture of the bishop, the priests show their intention to exercise their priesthood. For they were ordained to the priesthood and they participate in the Spirit that was given to the bishop" (introduction to the *Apostolic Tradition*, Sources Chrétiennes, 11bis, 26–27).

70 *Letter* 1980, no. 5.

the Church is the *sacramentum pietatis, signum unitatis, vinculum caritatis* (cf. Saint Augustine, *In Evangelium Ioannis* 26,13) form between us at this time a point or division and a source of distortion of thought and of behavior, instead of being the focal point and constitutive center, which it truly is in its essence, of the unity of the Church herself?[71]

The Eucharist—to which the priesthood instituted by Christ is essentially united to ensure its perpetuity—is, therefore, communion with Christ and source of unity for the baptized. Its celebration is also a manifestation of her unity, which it strengthens (cf. Acts 2:42). This communion of the people of God, which is called "ecclesial communion," is desired by its Divine Founder.

> This communion must be lived in compliance with the new commandment: "Love one another as I have loved you" (Jn 13:34). It is not by chance that the priestly prayer is the culmination of this "mystagogy" [on the gesture of the washing of the feet], since it shows us Christ in his oneness with the Father, ready to return to him through the sacrifice of himself, and wanting only that the disciples come to share his unity with the Father: "As you, Father, are in me and I in you, may they too be one in us" (Jn 17:21).
>
> From the small group of disciples who heard these words the whole Church was formed, growing through time and space as "a people gathered together by the unity of Father, Son and Holy Spirit" (Saint Cyprian, *De Orat. Dom.*, 23).[72]

Not only does John Paul II quote Saint Cyprian to express the unity toward which all the disciples of Jesus are decidedly oriented, but he also repeatedly cites the very strong and well-known expression of Saint Augustine: "Where I'm terrified by what I am for you, I am given comfort by what I am with you. For you I am a Bishop, with you, after all, I am a Christian. The first is the name of an office undertaken, the second a name of grace; that one means danger, this one salvation (*Serm.* 340,1)."[73] There is a fundamental unity and equal dignity among all those who have been regenerated by the waters of Baptism that Holy Orders in no way cancels or abrogates.

---

71 *Letter* 1980, Conclusion.

72 *Letter* 2000, nos. 4–5.

73 *Letters* 1979, no. 1; 1985, no. 2; 2001, no. 10.

These words of Saint Augustine also express a functional distinction: "For you I am a Bishop." This distinction, desired by Christ upon instituting the Twelve, is a service for the unity of the baptized. Also, quoting Saint Ignatius of Antioch, the pope makes us understand that this distinction is at the service of "hierarchical communion"[74] and the whole Church.

> The Second Vatican Council [. . .] also gave a new form to the life of the priestly communities, joined together by a special bond of brotherhood, and united to the Bishop of the respective local Church. The whole priestly life and ministry serve to deepen and strengthen that bond. [. . .] All this is meant to ensure that each Bishop, in Union with his Presbyterium, can serve ever more effectively the great cause of evangelization. Through this service the Church realizes her mission, indeed her very nature. The importance of the unity of the Priests with their own Bishop on this point is confirmed by the words of Saint Ignatius of Antioch: "Strive to do all things in the harmony of God, with the Bishop presiding to represent God, the presbyters representing the council of the apostles, and the deacons, so dear to me, entrusted with the service of Jesus Christ" (*Epistula ad Magnesios*, VI,1).[75]

This necessary communion finds its reason for being in the sacrament of Holy Orders, because "priests, prudent cooperators with the episcopal order, [. . .] constitute one priesthood with their bishop,"[76] and they share

---

74 This expression is used for the sole purpose of emphasizing the relationship between the bishop and the priests in the local church by analogy to the "hierarchical communion" referred to by the Second Vatican Council. Cf. *LG*, 21–22.

75 *Letter* 1979, no. 1.

76 *LG* 28. "*LG* 28 [rehabilitates] the ancient ecclesiology of communion, as well as the missionary perspective as a fundamental element in understanding the rationale of the ordained ministry, whose starting point is not the presbyterate but the episcopate. This is the perspective of *LG* 19–20, where the bishops are presented to us as the successors of the apostles, who in turn are the continuators of the mission that Jesus entrusted to them. [. . .] The priest, by virtue of the sacramental ordination that he has received, participates in the priesthood of Christ and, in view of the apostolic mission entrusted to him, he is invested with the triple power which puts him in a position to collaborate with the bishop in the building of the Church. [. . .] The decree *Presbyterorum ordinis* is influenced by this ecclesiological turn, as is also its vision of the episcopate as the origin of the priestly mission. In this perspective, he places the figure of the minister in the perspective of the mission (*PO* 2), applying the diagram of the three munera (*PO* 4–6) and recovering the theme of the presbyterium which emphasizes the collegial aspect of the Presbyteral Ministry. He posits the concept of pastoral charity as a unifying principle in the life of priests (*PO* 14) and insists on the common Christian vocation to holiness which, in the case of the ordained minister, manifests itself in the exercise of his pastoral ministry." Silvio Cajiao, "Le sacerdoce ministériel dans les documents de l'Église du Concile de Trente à Vatican II," Congregation for the Clergy, June 27, 2003, accessed September 13, 2021, www.clerus.org/clerus/ dati/2003-07/28-13/03SMFRA.html (translation mine).

the priesthood of Christ for the same mission. Indeed, "the ministerial priesthood took place within the context of a priestly community and communion. Jesus assembled the first group, that of the Twelve, and called them to form a union in mutual love. He wanted to join coworkers to this first 'priestly' community [and] he sent them out two by two."[77]

The Holy Spirit: *Scala ascensionis ad Deum*—Stairway of Our Ascent to God

The letters do not compose a systematic treatise of sacramental theology on the priesthood. As a result, themes reoccur and repeat, completing and deploying the pope's wealth of thought on the ministerial priesthood. However, some letters touch upon very specific topics, as in the case of the 1998 issue. Its theme is the Holy Spirit, and it contains the largest number of grouped quotations from the ecclesiastical authors, including from Saint Ireneaus, from whom is taken the title of this section, *Scala ascensionis ad Deum*.[78]

Indeed, the letter of Holy Thursday 1998 invites the priests to look toward Jesus, "who institutes the Eucharist and Holy Orders" but also "to contemplate the work of the Holy Spirit in us and to implore his gifts in order to conform ourselves all the more to Christ, the Priest of the New Covenant."[79] John Paul II affirms again that "the Eucharist and Orders are fruits of the same Spirit: 'As in the Mass it is he who works the transubstantiation of bread and wine into the Body and Blood of Christ, so in the Sacrament of Orders it is he who works the consecration of bishop or priest.' (*Gift and Mystery*, 53)"[80]

The pope appeals to the Fathers to ascertain the gifts of the Spirit infused into the soul of the baptized.

---

77 *General Audience*, August 4, 1993, no. 1.

78 Irenaeus, *Adv. Hæreses* III,24,1, quoted in *Letter* 1998, no. 6.

79 *Letter* 1998, introduction.

80 *Letter* 1998, no. 2. One can already understand the deep connection between the institution of the Eucharist on Holy Thursday and the gift of the Spirit, which will be discussed later in chapter 2. For, "as we ponder the birth of our Priesthood on this Holy Thursday, each of us recalls that most evocative moment when, on the day of our priestly Ordination, we prostrated ourselves on the sanctuary floor. This gesture of deep humility and obedient openness was splendidly designed to ready our soul for the sacramental imposition of hands, through which the Holy Spirit entered us to accomplish his work. Once we had risen from the floor, we knelt before the Bishop to be ordained priests and our hands were anointed by him for the celebration of the Holy Sacrifice, while the congregation chanted: 'living spring, fire, love, anointing of the soul'" (*Letter* 1998, no. 7).

Saint Irenaeus also makes mention of *the sevenfold gift* and adds: "God gave this same Spirit to the Church [. . .] sending the Consoler upon the earth" (*Adversus Haereses*, III, 17, 3). Saint Gregory the Great in turn illustrates the supernatural dynamic which the Spirit imparts to the soul, listing the gifts in inverse order: "Through the fear of the Lord we rise to piety, from piety then to knowledge, from knowledge we derive strength, from strength counsel, with counsel we move towards understanding and with intelligence towards wisdom and thus, by the sevenfold grace of the Spirit, there opens to us at the end of the ascent the entrance to the life of heaven" (*Hom. In Hezech.*, II, 7, 7).[81]

These gifts, offered to all who have been regenerated by Baptism, are ordained for the sanctification and perfection of the person.[82] However, "in order that they may exercise their demanding ministry with profit, the Spirit reserves special attention for those who have received Holy Orders."[83] By the gifts of the Comforter, which are "perfections of man which dispose him to follow readily the promptings of God,"[84] the ordained minister makes himself docile from the inside of his life and his being to the salvific work of God.[85]

With the *seven gifts*, the believer can enter into a personal and intimate relationship with the Father, with the freedom proper to the children of

---

[81] *Letter* 1998, no. 3.

[82] Cf. *CCC*, no. 1830–1831. "By the sacred Septenary, the Spirit thus guides the baptized to the full configuration of Christ and the total harmony with the perspectives of the Kingdom of God" (*Letter* 1998, no. 5).

[83] *Letter* 1998, no. 5. In fact "with the gift of *wisdom*, therefore, the Spirit leads the priest to evaluate all things in the light of the Gospel [. . .]; With the gift of *understanding*, the Spirit fosters in the priest a deeper insight into revealed truth, pressing him to proclaim with conviction and power the Good News of salvation. With the gift of *counsel*, the Spirit illuminates the ministry of Christ so that the priest may direct his activities according to the perspectives of Providence, never allowing himself to be swayed by the judgements of the world. With the gift of *strength*, the priest is sustained in the hardships of his ministry [. . .]; with the gift of *knowledge*, the priest is able to understand and accept the sometimes mysterious interweaving of secondary causes with the First Cause in the turn of events in the universe. With the gift of *piety*, the Spirit revives in the priest the relationship of intimate communion with God and of trusting surrender to his Providence. Finally, with the gift of *fear of the Lord*, last in the hierarchy of gifts, the Spirit gives the priest a stronger sense of his own human weakness and of the indispensable role of divine grace" (*Letter* 1998, no. 5, emphasis in the original).

[84] Saint Thomas, *Summa Theologiae* I-II, q. 68, a. 2, cited in *Letter* 1998, no. 4.

[85] Without doubt, "the Holy Spirit, as a gift to man, transforms the human world from within, from inside hearts and minds." John Paul II, Encyclical *Dominum et vivificantem* on the Holy Spirit in the Life of the Church and the World (May 18, 1986), no. 59.

God. This is what Saint Thomas underscores in noting how the Holy Spirit leads us to act not because we are compelled but because we love. "The Holy Spirit," he writes, "leads the children of God in freedom, through love, not by compulsion, through fear" (*Contra Gentiles*, Book IV, 22).[86]

"*The Holy Spirit directs the earthly life of Jesus towards the Father,*"[87] and the priest, configured to Christ by his ordination, is therefore also invited to direct his whole life toward the Trinitarian mystery: "We are also inspired to entrust ourselves to the action of the Spirit with a fresh heart and full receptiveness, allowing ourselves to be conformed day by day to Christ the priest."[88] In fact, in entrusting himself to His action, "the Paraclete, 'stairway of our ascent to God' (Saint Irenaeus, *Adversus Haereses*, III, 24, 1), draws the priest to the Father, stirring in his heart a burning desire to see God's face."[89]

Ars est artium regimen animarum—The Supreme Art Is the Direction of Souls

As I have discussed above, the ordained minister must personally direct his life to God, knowing that his mission is great, that his main task is to lead souls to the Lord.

> The priest [. . .] together with the faithful entrusted to his pastoral care, walks the path which leads to Christ! The priest yearns to come with them to a true knowledge of the Father and the Son, and so to pass from the experience of the Paraclete's action in history *per speculum in aenigmate* (1 Cor 13:12) to the contemplation of the living and pulsating reality of the Trinity *facie ad faciem* (1 Cor 13:12). He is well aware that he faces "a long crossing on little boats" and that he soars heavenwards "on little wings" (Saint Gregory of Nazianzus, *Theological Poems*, 1). But he can

---

86 *Letter* 1998, no. 4.

87 *Letter* 1998, no. 1, emphasis in the original.

88 *Letter* 1998, no. 2.

89 *Letter* 1998, no. 6. The pope continues: "The Paraclete makes known to him everything concerning the Son, drawing him to Christ with a deepening nostalgia; and the Paraclete illumines the priest about his own Person, that the priest may come to see the Spirit in his own heart and in history.

Therefore, among the joys and anxieties, the sufferings and hopes of the ministry, the priest learns to put his trust in the final victory of love, thanks to the unfailing action of the Spirit who, despite the limitations of men and institutions, leads the Church to live the mystery of unity and truth in its fullness."

also count on the One who set himself to teach the disciples everything (cf. Jn 14:26).[90]

For the ordained minister, "the supreme art is the direction of souls."[91] This expression, used by John Paul II to express the office of the ordained ministers, harbors the spirit that must animate the priest pastor's heart, which must be formed and strengthened.

> The special care for the salvation of others, for truth, for the love and holiness of the whole People of God, for the spiritual unity of the Church—this care that has been entrusted to us by Christ, together with the priestly power, is exercised in various ways. Of course there is a difference in the ways in which you, dear Brothers, fulfill your priestly vocation [. . .]. Nevertheless, within all these differences, *you are always and everywhere the bearers of your particular vocation*: you are bearers of the grace of Christ, the eternal Priest, and bearers of the charism of the Good Shepherd. And this you can never forget; this you can never renounce; this you must put into practice at every moment, in every place and in every way. In this consists that "supreme art" to which Jesus Christ has called you. "The supreme art is the direction of souls," wrote Saint Gregory the Great.
> I say to you therefore, quoting these words of his: strive to be "artists" of pastoral work. There have been many such in the history of the Church.[92]

By guiding souls to God, pastors lead to "green pastures" (Ps 23:2), the pope says, not to themselves. They cannot use their ministry to attract people to themselves, but they must be aware that they are "intermediaries," "facilitators" of the encounter between men and God, and that they must reveal the one who is *interior intimo meo* ("more inward than my innermost self"). In sum, they must reflect what they have profoundly become.

---

90 *Letter* 1998, no. 6.

91 Gregory the Great, *Regula pastoralis* 1,1, quoted in *Letter* 1979, no. 6.

92 *Letter* 1979, no. 6, which continues: "They speak to each of us, for example, Saint Vincent de Paul, Saint John of Avila, the holy Curé d'Ars, Saint John Bosco, Blessed Maximilian Kolbe, and many, many others. Each of them was different from the others, was himself, was the son of his own time and was 'up to date' with respect to his own time. But this 'bringing up to date' of each of them was an original response to the Gospel, a response needed precisely for those times; it was the response of holiness and zeal. There is no other rule apart from this for 'bringing ourselves up to date,' in our priestly life and activity, with our time and with the world as it is today. Without any doubt, the various attempts and projects aimed at the 'secularization' of the priestly life cannot be considered an adequate 'bringing up to date.'"

In Christ's way of acting there is one element which is very instructive. When the young man addresses Him ("Good Teacher"), *Jesus in a certain sense* puts Himself "to one side", because he replies: "No one is good but God alone." (Cf. Mt 19:17, Mk 10:17–22, Lk 18:18–23) [. . .] We cannot obscure Him "who alone is good," who is invisible and at the same time totally present: *Interior intimo meo*, as Saint Augustine says (*Conf.* III, VI, 11). Acting in the most natural manner, in the "first person," we cannot forget that the "first person" in every dialogue of salvation can only be *the One who alone saves and alone sacrifices.* [. . .] [O]ur pastoral work in whatever form [. . .] must serve in all humility to create and to *make more room for God*, for Jesus Christ.[93]

Ultimately, by all that he is in his human and spiritual qualities and in his deepest intentions, the priest must be a "bridge and not an obstacle for others in their meeting with Jesus Christ the Redeemer of humanity."[94]

THE CONCILIAR MAGISTERIUM

In examining the teaching that John Paul II inherited, I am not dwelling on the study of the pontifical magisterium preceding him. He quotes, in all these letters, the great pontiffs of the twentieth century.[95] However, I will not analyze this pontifical magisterium, because it seems to refer back to the Second Vatican Council—whose sources will be presented later—either because the council integrates it (Pius XII and John XXIII) or because the council's teaching is taken up again by theirs (Paul VI) and deepened by John Paul II himself. Therefore, I will focus on the councils—the Second Vatican Council chiefly, but first, the Council of Trent.

---

93 *Letter* 1985, no. 5, emphasis in the original.

94 John Paul II, Apostolic exhortation *Pastores dabo vobis* on the formation of priests in the circumstances of the present day (March 25, 1992), no. 43. Hereafter *PDV*.

95 Pius XII (Encyclical *Mystici Corporis*, June 29, 1943, quoted in *Letter* 1994, no. 3), John XXIII (Encyclical *Sacerdotii nostri primordia*, August 1, 1959, quoted in *Letter* 1986, no. 2), and especially Paul VI (Motu proprio *Ecclesiae Sanctae*, August 6, 1966, no. 2 and no. 8 and Encyclical *Sacerdotalis caelibatus*, June 24, 1967, quoted in *Letter* 1979, no. 1; Encyclical *Mysterium fidei*, September 3, 1965, quoted in *Letter* 1980, no. 3; *General Audience*, September 15, 1965, quoted in *Letter* 1980, no. 4; Apostolic Constitution *Missale Romanum*, April 3, 1969, quoted in *Letter* 1980, no. 10; Encyclical *Mysterium Fidei* quoted again in *Letter* 1980, no. 13; Encyclical *Humanae Vitae*, July 25, 1968, quoted in *Letter* 1994, no. 2; *Homily of Pentecost*, May 25, 1969, quoted in *Letter* 1998, no. 4).

The Council of Trent

John Paul II makes only four allusions to the Council of Trent (1545–1563). It is a small number of quotations, but he cites crucial definitions of the faith, formulated to reaffirm and propose again the Catholic doctrine on the sacraments of the Eucharist and the Holy Orders.[96]

The appeal to the Council of Trent and traditional Catholic teaching is not trivial. The first time the pope invokes it is in his letter of 1980, in a context where the identity of the priest is questioned and where the Eucharist seemed to be reduced, by some, to an ordinary "fraternal meal."[97] The priestly ministry is not a mere "function" but a true "consecration" of the very being of the one who receives the sacrament of Holy Orders. Indeed,

---

96 Indeed, the Council of Trent wanted to respond to the position of the reformers who proposed different theses. Among other things, they asserted that Holy Orders was not a sacrament, but simply a special rite designed to select and establish ministers of the Word. Consequently, according to them, Jesus would not have instituted the sacrament of Holy Orders; there would be no visible and external priesthood. This is a consequence of the negation of the Eucharist as the true sacrifice of Christ entrusted to the Church: there is no spiritual power to consecrate the Body and Blood of the Lord, to offer the sacrifice, or to forgive sins, but only the mandate and the ministry to proclaim the Gospel. To be a priest means only to exercise a ministry or office, and there is no difference from being baptized except the office. Cf. Benedetto Testa, *I sacramenti della Chiesa* (Milan: Jaca Book, 2001), 295–96.

    This is why the Council Fathers of Trent developed canons to affirm that in the new covenant there is a visible, external and particular priesthood, which has the power to consecrate the Body and Blood of Jesus Christ—truly present in the consecrated species—and to forgive sins. Because of this, ordination is a true sacrament, instituted by Christ, which gives the Holy Spirit. The priesthood is not an emanation of the community, but it is received by a consecration. The Council of Trent therefore confirmed the existence of the sacrament of the Holy Orders and defined it as a matter of faith, recalling that Christ linked the priesthood to the Eucharist: the priests are the successors of the Apostles in the priesthood while being distinct from the bishops. For a brief presentation of the sacraments of the Holy Orders and the Eucharist, according to the Tridentine perspective, see Bernard Sesboüé, *Les Signes du Salut*, vol. 3 of *Histoire des Dogmes* (Paris: Desclée, 1994), 158–70 and 184–92; for a quick overview of the Council of Trent, see also Giuseppe Alberigo, *Les Conciles Œcuméniques*, vol. 1 of *L'Histoire* (Paris: Cerf, 1994), 307–21. After the Council of Trent and given the historical context of the Counter-Reformation, the cultic and sacrificial aspect of the priesthood were honored more than the pastoral aspect.

97 "Perhaps in these recent years—at least in certain quarters—there has been too much discussion about the priesthood, the priest's 'identity,' the value of his presence in the modern world, etc., and on the other hand there has been too little praying" (*Letter* 1979, no. 10). In fact, "without any doubt, the various attempts and projects aimed at the 'secularization' of the priestly life cannot be considered an adequate 'bringing up to date' [. . .]. Those who call for the secularization of priestly life and applaud its various manifestations will undoubtedly abandon us when we succumb to temptation" (*Letter* 1979, nos. 6–7). Indeed "it is not at all a matter of 'laicizing' the clergy any more than it is a matter of 'clericalizing' the laity" (*Letter* 1989, no. 4).

by the proper grace of priestly ordination we are consecrated to offer the Eucharist: "The Eucharist is the principal and central *raison d'être* of the sacrament of the priesthood, which effectively came into being at the moment of the institution of the Eucharist, and together with it (cf. Ecumenical Council of Trent, sess. XXII, can. 2)."[98]

> We were born from the Eucharist. If we can truly say that the whole Church lives from the Eucharist ("*Ecclesia de Eucharistia vivit*"), as I reaffirmed in my recent Encyclical, we can say the same thing about the ministerial priesthood: it is born, lives, works and bears fruit "*de Eucharistia*" (cf. Ecumenical Council of Trent, sess. XXII, can. 2).[99]

In the Eucharist, the Church celebrates the greatest mystery of her faith, for "after the consecration of the bread and wine, our Lord Jesus Christ, true God and man, is truly, really, and substantially contained under the species of those sensible things."[100] He is present in a manner that can only be recognized in faith, for this sacrament is the memorial of the redeeming sacrifice and the paschal event. It is not therefore a mere spiritual presence of the Lord. John Paul II reiterates with profound faith:

> With deep emotion I am sending you this traditional Holy Thursday Letter, taking my seat beside you as it were at the table in the Upper Room at which the Lord Jesus celebrated with his Apostles the first Eucharist: a gift to the whole Church, a gift which, although veiled by sacramental signs, makes him "really, truly and substantially" present (Ecumenical Council of Trent, sess. XIII, can. 1) in every tabernacle throughout the world.[101]

---

98 *Letter* 1980, no. 2. Here is canon 2: "If any one shall say, that by those words, 'Do this in remembrance of me' (1 Cor 11:25, 1 Cor 11:24), Christ did not institute the apostles priests, or, did not ordain that they, and other priests, should offer His own body and blood: let him be anathema" (*DS* 1752). One can read in session XXIII, chap. 1, that "sacrifice and priesthood are, by the ordinance of God [that] the Catholic Church has received, from the institution of our Lord, the holy visible sacrifice of the Eucharist [and] a new priesthood" (*DS* 1764).

99 *Letter* 2004, no. 2. In *Letter* 1980, no. 2, he says: "Through our ordination [. . .] we are united in a singular and exceptional way to the Eucharist. In a certain way we derive from it and exist for it. We are also, and in a special way, responsible for it: [. . .] thus we bishops and priests are entrusted with the great 'mystery of Faith,' and while it is also given to the whole People of God, to all believers in Christ, yet to us has been entrusted the Eucharist also 'for' others, who expect from us a particular witness of veneration and love towards this sacrament."

100 Ecumenical Council of Trent, sess. XIII, chap. 1.

101 *Letter* 2002, no. 1.

Finally, again referring to the Council of Trent, the pope recalls that the Eucharist builds ecclesial communion.[102]

> This drawing together and this union, the prototype of which is the union of the Apostles about Christ at the Last Supper, express the Church and bring her into being.
>
> But the Church is not brought into being only through the union of people, through the experience of brotherhood to which the Eucharistic Banquet gives rise. The Church is brought into being when, in that fraternal union and communion, we celebrate the sacrifice of the cross of Christ, when we proclaim "the Lord's death until he comes" (1 Cor 11:26). [. . .] [T]he Church is being built up through that same communion with the Son of God, a communion which is a pledge of the eternal Passover [. . .] Therefore in Eucharistic Communion we receive Christ, Christ Himself; and our union with Him, which is a gift and grace for each individual, brings it about that in Him we are also associated in the unity of His body which is the Church.[103]

As already affirmed by John Paul II in his first encyclical, "the Eucharist builds the Church" and is her source of unity. Indeed, it marked her forever by this "unity that was shared by the Apostles and the first disciples of the Lord. The Eucharist builds ever anew this community and unity, ever building and regenerating it on the basis of the Sacrifice of Christ."[104]

---

102 It is a text that that has been already quoted and which is repeated here: "The doctrine of the Eucharist, sign of unity and bond of charity, taught by Saint Paul (cf. 1 Cor 10:17, commented by Saint Augustine, *In Evangelium Ioannis tract.*, 31,13, and by the Ecumenical Council of Trent, sess. XIII, chap. 8), has been in subsequent times deepened by the writings of very many saints" (*Letter* 1980, no. 5). Here is an excerpt from the text of Trent to which John Paul II refers: "This holy synod with fatherly affection admonishes, exhorts, entreats, and beseeches, by the bowels of the mercy of our God, that all and each of those who are reckoned under the Christian name, would now at length join and agree in this sign of unity, in this bond of charity, in this symbol of concord" (Ecumenical Council of Trent, sess. XIII, chap. 8). These remarks do not concern at first an ecumenical issue, but, according to the title itself, "On the Use of this Admirable Sacrament," it unites hearts to God and is a sign of communion between the faithful.

103 *Letter* 1980, no. 4. This paragraph broadly expands on the theme of the relationship between the Eucharist and ecclesial communion. The paragraph that follows will be summarized by reference to the Council of Trent and Augustine.

104 Encyclical *Redemptor Hominis* (March 4, 1979), no. 20. At the same time, the pope says: "[H]ow could the Eucharist, which in the Church is the *sacramentum pietatis, signum unitatis, vinculum caritatis* [sacrament of love, a sign of unity, a bond of charity], form between us at this time a point or division and a source of distortion of thought and of behavior, instead of being the focal point and constitutive center, which it truly is in its essence, of the unity of the Church herself? [. . .] In the name of this truth and of this love, in the name of the crucified Christ and of

The Second Vatican Council

It is now appropriate to study the magisterium of the Second Vatican Council as the source of the Letters of Holy Thursday. John Paul II draws heavily on it, either by referring to it or by quoting excerpts from it.

In all, seven conciliar documents are quoted: the dogmatic constitutions *Lumen Gentium*,[105] *Gaudium et Spes*,[106] and *Sacrosanctum Concilium*,[107] as well as the decrees *Presbyterorum Ordinis*,[108] *Optatam Totius*,[109] *Ad gentes*,[110] and *Unitatis redintegratio*.[111]

For this study, not all the texts are equally pertinent. Thus, I will deal only with the texts most quoted by the pope. On these instances the subjects of special interest to the Holy Father are discussed, namely, *Lumen Gentium* 10,[112] 11,[113] and 28.[114]

The Dogmatic Constitution *Lumen Gentium*

Three themes gathered from the quotes of the dogmatic constitution about the Church, *Lumen Gentium*, can be identified: first, the difference and the correlation between the common priesthood and the hierarchical priesthood (no. 10);[115] next, the Eucharist as the source and summit of the life of

---

His Mother, I ask you, and beg you: Let us abandon all opposition and division, and let us all unite in this great mission of salvation which is the price and at the same time the fruit of our redemption" (*Letter* 1980, no. 13).

105 *Lumen Gentium* is the most quoted text in paragraphs 3, 4, 7, 10, 11, 13, 18, 26, 28, 34, 35, 36, 37, 48, 58, and 64.

106 Paragraphs 2, 22, 38, 39, and 42.

107 Paragraphs 2, 7, 10, 35, 47, and 51.

108 After *Lumen Gentium*, the decree *Presbyterorum Ordinis* is the most cited conciliar document. Paragraphs 2, 3, 4, 5, 6, 9, 10, 12, and 13.

109 Paragraph 22.

110 Paragraphs 9, 13, and 19.

111 Paragraphs 2 and 15.

112 Paragraph quoted nine times. It deals, in chapter 2, which is devoted to the "People of God," with the "royal priesthood."

113 Cited seven times. This paragraph of chapter 2 treats the exercise of the common priesthood in the sacraments.

114 Paragraph quoted five times. It is located in chapter 3, on the hierarchical constitution of the Church, and treats of the priests in their relation to Christ, the bishops, the presbyterium, and the Christian people.

115 *Letters* 1979, nos. 3, 4, 5; 1989, no. 2; 1990, no. 3; 1995, no. 6; 2000, no. 7.

the Church (no. 11);[116] and finally, the pastoral mission of ordained ministers (no. 28).[117]

Following paragraph 10, first, it should be recalled that

> the priesthood in which we share through the sacrament of Orders, which
> has been for ever "imprinted" on our souls through a special sign from
> God, that is to say the "character," remains in explicit relationship with the
> common priesthood of the faithful, that is to say the priesthood of all the
> baptized, but at the same time it differs from that priesthood "essentially
> and not only in degree" (*LG* 10).[118]

These words of John Paul II affirm, following the Council, that "*the
universal priesthood of the faithful and the royal dignity* belong to both
men and women,"[119] and "the entire People of God participates in this
priesthood by Baptism."[120] In fact, Christ associates baptized people with
his priesthood and with his prophetic and royal mission. In this way, He
continues to live in the Church and to act through it in the world.[121] Christ
acts not from the outside but from the inside, because He pursues His
mission through each member of this consecrated community.[122]
Whoever enters the Church through Baptism receives this sacerdotal consecration. The Council designates this priesthood as "common priest-

---

116 *Letters* 1980, nos. 1, 4; 1982, no. 1; 1986, no. 8; 1987, no. 12; 2000, no. 5.

117 *Letters* 1980, no. 1, 9; 1986, no. 8; 1989, no. 6; 1990, no. 3.

118 *Letter* 1979, no. 3.

119 *Letter* 1995, no. 6, emphasis in the original.

120 *Letter* 2000, no. 7.

121 "The constitution follows the tripartite division of the function of Christ: Priest, Prophet
or Master, and King or Pastor. In chapter II this triple division is applied to the whole people
of the new Covenant (nos. 10–12)" (Bertulf Van Leeuwen, "La participation universelle à la
fonction prophétique du Christ," p. 426). On the other hand, "before speaking of the hierarchy, [the constitution] deals with the People of God and his universal priesthood. It is only
further that it deals with the *dona propria* (*particular gifts*), particular vocations and functions
found within the Catholic community. [. . .] The hierarchical functions appear in the Constitution (chapter III) as a special, specific, and particularly important form of these *dona propria*
in the universal priesthood." Émile-Joseph de Smedt, "Le sacerdoce des fidèles," *Unam sanctam* 51b (1966): 412.

122 Indeed "Christ [. . .] was consecrated priest . . . mediator, charged with fulfilling in himself
the perfect passage to the Father, opening the door to us and leading us to follow him. [. . .]
The Church . . . is one with Him and continues His Work of Passage to the Father." Léon Etienne
Duval et al., *L'Église: Constitution "Lumen gentium." Texte conciliaire: introduction, commentaires* (Paris: Mame, 1965), 71.

hood"[123] because it is universal—that is to say, it is common to all the faithful—and it is the condition of all subsequent consecration.

The pope also says that "the Second Vatican Council reminds us that, in addition to the participation proper [in the priesthood of Christ] to all the baptized, there exists another specific, ministerial participation which, although intimately linked to the first, nonetheless differs from it in essence (cf. *LG* 10)."[124] This distinction is therefore deeper than the difference between the diaconate, the priesthood, and the episcopate.[125]

Indeed, the *sacerdotium ministeriale seu hierarchicum*—the ministerial or hierarchical priesthood[126]—is a service by which Christ places at the disposal of his disciples the means to accomplish their mission. It is for this reason that the exercise of the ministerial priesthood is always directed to

---

123 *LG* 10. Without any doubt, "*Lumen Gentium* clearly affirmed, as never a document of the Magisterium had done, the priesthood common to all baptized. That every man participating in the life and condition of Jesus, Man-God is himself consecrated and in priestly condition is one of the clearest, the most new and probably the most important of Vatican II's affirmations." Jean Vilnet, "Orientations doctrinales du Concile," *Vocation* 233 (1966): 225.

124 *Letter* 2000, no. 7.

125 In fact, "the ministerial priesthood differs in essence from the common priesthood of the faithful because it confers a sacred power for the service of the faithful. The ordained ministers exercise their service for the People of God by teaching (*munus docendi*), divine worship (*munus liturgicum*) and pastoral governance (*munus regendi*)" (*CCC*, no. 1592). "It had been proposed to speak of analogical resemblance. The Council did not retain this theological terminology, but the description given of the relationship between the two priesthoods corresponds to what we are accustomed to call analogical resemblance: 'They are, however, ordered one to the other; for both of them participate, each in a particular way, in the unique priesthood of Christ'" (Smedt, "Le sacerdoce des fidèles," 414). This choice of the Council Fathers seems sensible, because the common priesthood of the faithful is not a metaphor, nor a derivation of the hierarchical ministerial priesthood. This is not an *analogatum princeps* for the common priesthood of believers, because it derives from Baptism and its model from the one priesthood of Christ, priest, prophet, and king.

126 One can say that "as a specific feature of the *sacerdotium ministeriale* (*ministerial priesthood*), the Constitution mentions that the latter implies a *sacra potestas* (*sacred power*), which it has the task of forming and directing (*efformat et regit*) the priestly people, which it has been established to fulfill (*conficit*) the Eucharistic sacrifice, in the name of the person of Christ, and to offer it (*offert*) in the name of the whole People of God. The emphasis is on the *specialis potestas*, through which the ministerial priesthood is empowered to act as a mediator: as a representative of Christ, and of all the Christian people. Although it is true that this representative mission, Christ did not entrust it to the universal priesthood; it remains that the latter confers a special mission. It empowers the faithful to take an active part in religious acts that have a sacred and community character. It is a common celebration of the Eucharist, of the frequentation of the sacraments, of prayer and thanksgiving in union with Christ, of the testimony of a life dedicated to holiness, of self-denial, and self-forgetfulness and finally effective and active charity (*actuosa caritas*) (cf. *LG* 10)." Smedt, "Le sacerdoce des fidèles," 412–13).

the universal priesthood of the people of God. For the ministerial priesthood is to be practiced in the manner of Jesus Christ (cf. *PO 2*).[127]

> We must consider down to the smallest detail not only the theoretical meaning but also the existential meaning of the mutual "relation" that exists between the hierarchical priesthood and the common priesthood of the faithful. The fact that they differ not only in degree but also in essence is a fruit of a particular aspect of the richness of the very priesthood of Christ, which is the one centre and the one source both of that participation which belongs to all the baptized and of that other participation which is reached through a distinct sacrament, which is precisely the sacrament of Orders. This sacrament, [. . .] by virtue of its very nature and of everything that it produces in our life and activity, serves to make the faithful aware of their common priesthood and to activate it: the sacrament reminds them that they are the People of God and enables them "to offer spiritual sacrifices" (cf. 1 Pt 2:5), through which Christ himself makes us an everlasting gift to the Father (cf. LG 10).[128]

Furthermore, "the universal priesthood is also essentially oriented towards the ministerial priesthood. Without the dispensation of the graces, the preaching of the Word, and the pastoral direction ensured by the hierarchy, the members of the universal priesthood would be deprived of the competence and the help that Christ wants to offer them by the Holy Spirit."[129]

---

127 The priest "must be very near to them [laity], as John Mary Vianney was, but as a priest, always in a perspective which is that of their salvation and of the progress of the kingdom of God. He is the witness and dispenser of a life other than earthly life. It is essential to the Church that the identity of the priest be safeguarded, with its vertical dimension" (*Letter* 1986, no. 10).

128 *Letter* 1979, no. 4. The text continues: "Conscious of this reality, we understand how our priesthood is 'hierarchical,' that is to say, connected with the power of forming and governing the priestly people (*LG* 10), and *precisely for this reason, 'ministerial.'* We carry out this office, through which Christ himself unceasingly 'serves' the Father in the work of our salvation. Our whole priestly existence is and must be deeply imbued with this service if we wish to effect in an adequate way the Eucharistic Sacrifice *in persona Christi.*" Emphasis in the original. Also, in his *Letter* 1990, no. 3, John Paul II said: "The priesthood is not an institution that exists 'alongside' the laity, or 'above' it. The priesthood of bishops and priests, as well as the ministry of deacons, is *'for' the laity*, and precisely for this reason it possesses a 'ministerial' character, that is to say one 'of service.' Moreover, it highlights the 'baptismal priesthood,' the priesthood common to all the faithful. It highlights this priesthood and at the same time helps it to be realized in the sacramental life."

129 Smedt, "Le sacerdoce des fidèles," 414. Moreover, as faithful and members of the people of God, the clergy themselves as such cannot do without the support of the ministerial priesthood.

When John Paul II appeals to no. 11 of *Lumen Gentium*, he uses only one sentence of this text: the "Eucharistic sacrifice [. . .] is the fount and apex of the whole Christian life"[130] because, indeed, the Eucharist is "a single sacrifice that embraces everything. It is the greatest treasure of the Church. It is her life." This paragraph of the conciliar constitution is entitled "The exercise of the common priesthood in the sacraments." However, far from being limited to an exclusive reference to the universal priesthood, the pope sees in the Eucharist the place of convergence of the common priesthood and the hierarchical priesthood: "Our eucharistic worship, both in the celebration of Mass and in our devotion to the Blessed Sacrament, is like a life-giving current that links our ministerial or hierarchical priesthood to the common priesthood of the faithful."[131]

The Eucharist is "source and summit" of the Christian life, and "eucharistic worship is the center and goal of all sacramental life,"[132] because the Church finds in it the heart of her mystery, which is also *sacramentum unitatis*.[133] In the Eucharist—which is communion between men and God and also the communion of men between themselves—the Church finds the source of her unity, the summit of the manifestation of the unity of the people of God, as well as the force for his mission in the world.[134]

> Thanks to the Council we have realized with renewed force the following truth: Just as the Church "makes the Eucharist" so "the Eucharist builds up" the Church (16) [. . .] through that same communion with the Son of God [. . .]. Only in this way, [. . .] is there brought about that building up of the Church, which in the Eucharist truly finds its "source and summit" (cf. *LG* 11). [. . .] Let all pastoral activity be nourished by it, and may it also be food for ourselves and for all the priests who collaborate with us, and likewise for the whole of the communities entrusted to us. In this practice there should thus be revealed, almost at every step, that close relationship between the Church's spiritual and apostolic vitality and the Eucharist.[135]

---

130 *Letter* 1982, no. 1.

131 *Letter* 1980, no. 2.

132 *Letter* 1980, no. 7.

133 Cf. Jean-Louis Witte, "L'Église *sacramentum unitatis* du cosmos et du genre humain," *Unam sanctam* 51b (1966): 461.

134 Cf. Marie-Joseph Le Guillou, "La vocation missionnaire de l'Église," *Unam sanctam* 51b (1966): 693.

135 *Letter* 1980, no. 4.

Finally, I have to consider the use of *Lumen Gentium* 28. This paragraph is important because of its history and its doctrinal density.[136] However, John Paul II will cite only short excerpts to express the relationship between priests and the Christian people, that is, their pastoral mission. This is a "*social task which is linked with his vocation as a pastor,* that is to say, he can 'gather together' the Christian communities to which he is sent. The council on several occasions emphasizes this task. [The] priests 'exercising the function of Christ, [. . .] *gather together God's family* as a brotherhood all of one mind and lead them in the Spirit, through Christ, to God the Father' (*LG* 28)."[137] This mission of assembly is accomplished by preeminence and manifests itself in all its fullness during the celebration of the Eucharist,[138] since "the Second Vatican Council says to us today on the subject of priests: 'They exercise this sacred function of Christ most of all in the Eucharistic Liturgy' (*LG* 28)."[139]

SYNTHESIS

At the end of this journey on Tradition and the Magisterium as sources for the *Letters to Priests* and of John Paul II's reflection on the priesthood, recurring themes that converge on the key concept of communion can be seen.

---

136 In fact, "*LG* 28, which is devoted to the ordained priesthood, has undergone a lot of modifications since its writing. It expresses more clearly that the ministerial priesthood has at its source the priesthood of Christ; here the question about the origin of the power of jurisdiction of priests is often avoided. It specifies that they also participate in the threefold priestly function of teaching, governing, and sanctifying. The text also contains a term 'render present—*repraesentant*,' dating from the Council of Trent and the report explains that this word means *praesentem reddere*." Boaventura Kloppenburg, "Votes et derniers amendements de la constitution," *Unam sanctam* 51b (1966): 461. On this paragraph one can read with profit the commentary of Karl Rahner, *La gerarchia nella Chiesa: commento al capitolo III di Lumen gentium* (Brescia: Morcelliana, 2008): 70–81. On its genesis, see Oswaldo Gandin, *A participação dos presbíteros na missão apostólica* (Rome: Atteneo Romano della Santa Croce, 1991): 63–99.

137 *Letter* 1989, no. 6. The pope says: "The pastoral vocation of priests is great, and the Council teaches that it is universal: it is directed towards the whole Church (*PO* 3, 6, 10, and 12); and therefore it is of a missionary character" (*Letter* 1979, no. 8).

138 See *Letter* 1980, no. 1.

139 *Letter* 1986, no. 8. Jean Giblet comments, "If the presbyters have the essential task of gathering and feeding the Church which is the flock of the only Pastor, they are also and correlatively the ministers of the New Covenant (*LG* 28). [. . .] One, therefore, resumes the traditional doctrine that has always emphasized the close connection of the priesthood with the Eucharistic sacrifice. The Constitution refers in this respect to the teachings of the Council of Trent and Pius XII. But it is important to note the perspective in which the doctrine is presented. The priesthood appears at the union of the sacrifice of Christ and of the faithful, as the instrument of the progressive realization of this perfect communion which will find its fulfillment in the Parousia." Jean Giblet, "Les prêtres," *Unam sanctam* 51c (1966): 931.

This notion—paramount at the Second Vatican Council—has a strong ecclesial connotation, and from it emerges the distinction of functions in the body of the Church (1 Cor 12:27–31). Thus, Tradition and the Magisterium unanimously testify that the ordained minister is consecrated by the anointing of the Spirit for the service of directing souls, offering them the goods of salvation. As a member of the body of Christ, like all the baptized, the priest is chosen to contribute in a unique way to its edification, promoting communion between the faithful and the hierarchical communion, and above all communion with God. This ecclesial communion manifests itself par excellence in the Eucharistic celebration.

At the beginning of this chapter, I said that the Holy Father did not intend to make a treatise on the priesthood with the letters of Holy Thursday, referring, for example, to the theological works that have traced the evolution of thought on this subject. However, one could have expected references to other authors and books that have emphasized this topic, especially John Chrysostom and Thomas Aquinas.

One theological work of John Chrysostom that might have merited a reference is *On the Priesthood*. It was written between 386 AD and 392 AD and is dedicated to Basil. It deals with life and pastoral ministry. It refers equally to priests and bishops, to whom he addresses the charge of priestly ministry in the aspects of government, teaching, and the presidency of worship. In this work, a complete presentation of the rite of ordination can also be found.[140] Of course, all this is presented according to a very high sacral vision of ordained ministry proper to the author.

As for Thomas Aquinas, his commentary on the *Sentences of Peter Lombard* draws attention. It is his most comprehensive treatise on ordained ministries, in which he presents the purpose of Holy Orders as oriented to the Eucharist. He also lays down the doctrine on the *potestas ordinis* and the *potestas iurisdictionis*,[141] concepts taken up and deepened during the Second Vatican Council. In the Tridentine context, these notions made it possible to focus the priestly consideration on the figure of the priest, given his power to offer the sacrifice, while the bishop differs from him only by a greater jurisdiction.

---

140 Cf. Joseph Lecuyer, *Le sacrement de l'ordination. Recherche historique et théologique* (Paris: Beauchesne, 1983): 105–14.

141 About the question of power of order and power of jurisdiction, see chapter 2, note 109.

Chapter 2

The Identity of the Priest

The first part of this book allowed us to go to the sources of John Paul II's reflection on the priestly ministry. It draws on the deposit of faith—the Holy Scriptures, Tradition, and the Magisterium—to present the Catholic priesthood in its relationship to Christ and to the Church.[1] It is therefore fitting in this chapter to question the identity of the priest as presented by the pope.[2]

EX HOMINIBUS ET PRO OMNIBUS—FROM MEN AND TO ALL

Ex hominibus assumptus—Chosen from among Men . . .

The title of this subdivision expresses a basic affirmation of the Catholic teaching included in the magisterium of John Paul II[3]: the priest, by his Baptism, is above all a faithful Christian, chosen from among his brothers.[4] Indeed,

> this very same priesthood of Christ is shared by everyone in the Church through the Sacrament of Baptism. Although the words "a priest chosen from among men" are applied to each of us who shares in the ministerial priesthood, they refer first of all to membership in the messianic people, in the royal priesthood. They point to *our roots in the common*

---

1 Cf. *CCC*, no. 86.

2 The post-synodal apostolic exhortation *Pastores dabo vobis* of March 25, 1992, states that the question of the priest's identity crisis is closed: "This crisis arose in the years immediately following the Council. It was based on an erroneous understanding of—and sometimes even a conscious bias against—the doctrine of the conciliar magisterium. [. . .] It is as though the 1990 synod—rediscovering [. . .] the full depth of priestly identity [. . .]—has striven to instill hope in the wake of these sad losses" (*PDV* 11). Thus, "from the question of the priest's identity [we proceed to the question] connected with the process of formation for the priesthood and the quality of priestly life" (*PDV* 3).

3 *Letter* 1979, no. 3.

4 The Holy Father remains in harmony with the perspective of the Letter to the Hebrews and the thought of the Second Vatican Council, mentioned in the first chapter.

priesthood of the faithful, which lies at the base of our individual call to the priestly ministry.[5]

The whole Church is associated with the priesthood of Christ, and that is why all the baptized participate in His unique priesthood: the Church is "the priestly people," as affirmed by the Second Vatican Council.[6] However, the priesthood of Christ is exercised in two different forms, either by the common priesthood or by the ministerial priesthood: "Each of them in its own special way is a participation in the one priesthood of Christ,"[7] and all of God's people have equal dignity by virtue of common baptismal regeneration.[8] One can also recall the beautiful doctrinal synthesis contained in the Preface of the Chrism Mass.

For by the anointing of the Holy Spirit you made your Only Begotten Son High Priest of the new and eternal covenant, and by your wondrous design were pleased to decree that His one Priesthood should continue in the Church. For Christ not only adorns with a royal priesthood the people He has made His own, but with a brother's kindness He also chooses men to become sharers in His sacred ministry through the laying on of hands.[9]

5 *Letter* 1989, no. 3, emphasis in the original.

6 Cf. *LG* 10. *Pastores dabo vobis* states: "In the rebirth of baptism, the Spirit of the Lord is poured out on all believers, consecrating them as a spiritual temple and a holy priesthood" (*PDV* 18).

7 *LG* 10. The *CCC*, no. 1141, affirms: "This 'common priesthood' is that of Christ the sole priest, in which all his members participate." According to statements made by Cardinal Christoph Schönborn on September 28, 2009, at the International Retreat for Priests (September 27–October 3, 2009, Ars, France), "the Council lists seven 'fields' of participation in the priesthood of Christ in which [the royal priesthood] can and must be deployed: first, as for the ministerial priesthood, there is participation in the offering of the Eucharist, the sacrifice of Christ and his Church inseparably. The reception of the sacraments is the second 'field of practice' of the royal priesthood. *LG* 11 unfolds in an admirable synthesis how each of the sacraments is received as a new actuation of the common priesthood of the baptized. The third and fourth fields follow the life of prayer and the thanksgiving by which Christ can bring His life into our own. Fifth field: *testimonio vitae sanctae*, by the witness of a holy life all the baptized exercise their participation in the priesthood of Christ. Sixth: the renunciations, lived after Christ, are like narrow doors through which Christ makes us pass from the old man to the new life of the children of God. And, seventh, the vast field of 'effective charity' in which all dimensions of human life can be penetrated by the transformative force of Christ's charity and make us 'homes of charity.'"

8 Cf. *LG* 32.

9 *Roman Missal.*

The common priesthood of the Christian people is a truth revealed in the New Testament writings.[10] This common priesthood, according to several Fathers of the Church, is intrinsically linked to Baptism and the anointing of the Spirit who consecrates the baptized as priests.[11] The Fathers call the priesthood of the faithful "spiritual priesthood." But for them, it is not a metaphorical or symbolic priesthood. It is "spiritual" because it is closely related to the action of the Holy Spirit, and truly sacramental because it is founded on the sacraments of Baptism and Confirmation. For this reason, it is a true and real priesthood.[12] Despite a certain obscuration in history,[13] this doctrine was constant in the teaching of the Church and has now entered the documents of the Magisterium.[14]

John Paul II summarizes what I have just affirmed about the common priesthood with strong and condensed words.

All [the baptized] *share in the priesthood of Christ,* and this sharing signifies that, already through Baptism "of water and the Holy Spirit" (Jn 3:5),

---

10 In his first epistle, Peter exalts the dignity of the Christian people and attests that, by divine mercy, they are "a chosen race, a royal priesthood, a holy nation" (1 Pt 2:9). With Christ, the living stone, the baptized are also "living stones built into a spiritual house to be a holy priesthood to offer spiritual sacrifices acceptable to God through Jesus Christ" (1 Pt 2:5). Referring to 1 Pt 2:9, John Paul II states: "[E]veryone in the Church—the people who by Baptism participate in Christ's priestly function—possesses the common 'royal priesthood' of which the Apostle Peter speaks (cf. 1 Pt 2:9)" (*Letter* 1988, no. 4).

Cf. also Rev 1:6; 5:10; 20:6. It is interesting to note that in the apocalyptic texts, John attributes to each Christian the priestly dignity and affirms that Christians are "priests." For a study on these texts, see Albert Vanhoye, *Old Testament Priests and the New Priest According to the New Testament* (Petersham: Saint Bede's Publications, 1986): 188–236.

Other passages of the New Testament, even if they do not speak explicitly of "priesthood," use an implicitly priestly language. For example: Jn 4:23; 1 Cor 3:16–17; 6:19–20; Rom 12:1; Heb 13:15–16.

11 Cf. John Chrysostom, *In II ad Corinthios epistulam*, PG 61, 417–18; Jerome, *Dialogus contra Luciferianos*, PL 23,166A; Augustine, *De civitate Dei*, XX,10; PL 41, 676.

12 This "spiritual" priesthood empowers the believer to participate and offer the Eucharistic Sacrifice.

13 This obscuration came about especially after the Council of Trent, which, in the face of Protestantism, pledged to defend the ministerial priesthood. The Catechism of the Council of Trent, published by Pius V in 1566, does not forget to speak of the common priesthood as *interius* and of the ministerial priesthood as *externum*. Cf. José Saraiva Martins, *Il sacerdozio ministeriale* (Rome: Pontificia Università Urbaniana, 1991), 57.

14 Cf. Pius XI, Encyclical *Miserentissimus Redemptor* (May 8, 1928); Pius XII, Encyclicals *Mystici Corporis* (June 29, 1943) and *Mediator Dei* (November 20, 1947). Vatican II gives the common priesthood great importance and treats this teaching in a broad and orderly way, emphasizing its reality, its nature, and its exercise, as well as its link with the ministerial priesthood: cf. *Lumen Gentium* 10–11, 34, 62; *Apostolicam Actuositatem* 2–3; *Ad Gentes* 15; *Presbyterorum Ordinis* 2.

they are consecrated to offer spiritual sacrifices in union with the one redeeming sacrifice offered by Christ himself. In him all become a "royal priesthood" as the messianic people of the new Covenant (1 Pet 2:9).[15]

The pope also emphasizes the Eucharistic orientation of the baptismal priesthood. He takes up a deeply patristic vision,[16] speaking of the Eucharist as the rendezvous place par excellence between the ministerial and baptismal priesthood.

> From this concept of eucharistic worship there then stems the whole sacramental style of the Christian's life. In fact, leading a life based on the sacraments and animated by the common priesthood means in the first place that Christians desire God to act in them in order to enable them to attain, in the Spirit, "the fullness of Christ himself." (Eph 4:13). [. . .] [O]f all the sacraments it is the Holy Eucharist that [. . .] confers upon the exercise of the common priesthood that sacramental and ecclesial form that links it [. . .] to the exercise of the ministerial priesthood.[17]

On this subject, the Holy Father once more expresses:

> In this way our eucharistic worship, both in the celebration of Mass and in our devotion to the Blessed Sacrament, is like a life-giving current that links our ministerial or hierarchical priesthood to the common priesthood of the faithful, and presents it in its vertical dimension and with its central value. The priest fulfills his principal mission and is manifested in all his fullness when he celebrates the Eucharist, and this manifestation is more complete when he himself allows the depth of that mystery to become visible, so that it alone shines forth in people's hearts and minds, through his ministry. This is the supreme exercise of the "kingly priesthood," "the source and summit of all Christian life" (LG 11).[18]

---

15 *Letter* 1989, no. 1.

16 The link between the baptismal priesthood and the Eucharistic Sacrifice is emphasized by many Fathers. Cf. Justin, *Dialogus cum Tryphone Judaeo*, 116, PG 6,745A; Origen, *In Leviticum*, hom. 9,9, *PG* 12,521C; Ambrose, *De Sacramentis*, PL 16,456B-457D; John Chrysostom, *In II ad Corinthios epistulam*, hom. 18, *PG* 61,527; Augustine, *De civitate Dei* X,20, PL 41,298; Cyril of Alexandria, *De adoratione in Spiritu et Veritate* XII, PG 68,833D-836A. The Eucharistic Sacrifice is not an exclusive affair of the ordained minister, but of the whole ecclesial community.

17 *Letter* 1980, no. 7.

18 *Letter* 1980, no. 2. In this same *Letter* he says, at no. 9: "The celebrant, as minister of this sacrifice, is the authentic priest, performing—in virtue of the specific power of sacred ordination—a true sacrificial act that brings creation back to God. Although all those who participate

Finally, coming back to *Lumen Gentium* 10, John Paul II unifies the ministerial and baptismal priesthood in an eminently cultic perspective:[19] "The faithful indeed, by virtue of their royal priesthood, participate in the offering of the Eucharist. They exercise that priesthood, too, by the reception of the sacraments, prayer and thanksgiving, the witness of a holy life, abnegation, and active charity."[20] It is now time to examine the question of their distinction. Because if it is necessary to affirm the existence of two forms of participation in the priesthood of Christ, it is all the more necessary to specify the difference.

Pro hominibus constituitur—. . . to Act on Behalf of Men

To the question just asked, John Paul II gives a beginning of an answer by recalling that the ministerial priesthood is "appointed to act on behalf of men,"[21] hence its distinction of the baptismal priesthood.

> The Second Vatican Council pointed out *the difference between the common priesthood* of all the baptized and the *priesthood* which we receive in the Sacrament of Orders. The Council calls the latter the "ministerial priesthood," which means both "office" and "service." It is also "hierarchical" in the sense of sacred service. For "hierarchy" means sacred governance, which in the Church is service.
>
> We recall the often-quoted *conciliar text*: "Though they differ from one another in essence and not only in degree, the common priesthood of the faithful and the ministerial or hierarchical priesthood are nonetheless interrelated: each of them in its own special way is a participation in the one priesthood of Christ. The ministerial priest, by the sacred power he

---

in the Eucharist do not confect the sacrifice as He does, they offer with Him, by virtue of the common priesthood, their own spiritual sacrifices represented by the bread and wine from the moment of their presentation at the altar." A hyphen between "of" and "sacred ordination" has been deleted from the official Vatican translation, as it seems to have been a mistake.

19 LG 10 affirms the essential difference of two kinds of priesthood but highlights what unites them as well as the equal dignity of the baptized. The document goes on to say that the baptized have received "the baptismal character for the worship of the Christian religion" (*LG* 11; cf. also *LG* 34), and they "share also in Christ's prophetic office" (*LG* 12). In addition to being the teaching of Vatican II, it is also the perspective of Saint Thomas Aquinas, according to Saraiva Martins, *Il sacerdozio ministeriale*, 56: "Participation in the priesthood of Christ [is] a deputation of the baptized to divine worship."

20 LG 10, cited in *Letter* 1979, no. 3.

21 Heb 5:1, cited in *Letter* 1979, no. 3. Cf. in chapter 1 the commentary made by John Paul II on the Letter to the Hebrews.

enjoys, teaches and rules the priestly people; acting in the person of Christ (*in persona Christi*), he makes present the Eucharistic sacrifice, and offers it to God in the name of all the people."[22]

The statement is clear: the baptismal priesthood and the hierarchical priesthood "differ from one another in essence and not only in degree."[23] John Paul II comments, "The fact that they differ not only in degree but also in essence is a fruit of a particular aspect of the richness of the very priesthood of Christ, which is the one centre and the one source both of that participation which belongs to all the baptized and of that other participation which is reached through a distinct sacrament, which is precisely the sacrament of Orders."[24] The baptized who receive this sacrament participate in the unique priesthood of Christ in a "new and special," "specific and authoritative way."[25] There is a "specific ontological bond which unites the priesthood to Christ,"[26] which makes the priest a "visible continuation and sacramental sign of Christ in his own position before the Church and the world, as the enduring and ever new source of salvation."[27] The pope notes that "in this way, the words of the author of the Letter to the Hebrews about the priest, who has been 'chosen from among men [. . .] appointed to act on behalf of men,' take on their full meaning."[28]

Vatican II renders a close link by affirming that "the common priesthood of the faithful and the ministerial or hierarchical priesthood are nonetheless interrelated"[29] because, indeed, since they derive from Christ's unique priest-

---

22 *Letter* 1989, no. 2.

23 This formula *essentia et non gradu tantum* is of scholastic origin and has been received in the Magisterium. The Council takes it up from Pius XII, who used it in his *Magnificate Dominum* speech of November 2, 1954. The *Directory of the Ministry and Life of the Priests*, no. 18, states that the distinction between the common priesthood and the ministerial priesthood is a "firm doctrine of the Church." On the question, I refer to the study of Antonio Acerbi, "Osservazioni sulla formula *essentia et non gradu tantum* nella dottrina cattolica sul sacerdozio," *Lateranum* 47 (1981): 98–101.

24 *Letter* 1979, no. 4. It is a distinction *ex divina institutione* (by divine institution), as the *Code of Canon Law* affirms in canon 207, §1: "By divine institution, there are among the Christian faithful in the Church sacred ministers."

25 *PDV* 15, 16.

26 *PDV* 11.

27 *PDV* 16.

28 *Letter* 1979, no. 3, citing Heb 5:1.

29 *LG* 10. John Paul II affirms that "we must consider down to the smallest detail not only the theoretical meaning but also the existential meaning of the mutual 'relation' that exists between

hood, it follows that between them there is an immanent reciprocal relationship. Thus, the ministerial priesthood is realized in the fruitful milieu of the
priesthood of all the baptized and is at the service of it. The latter, in turn,
unfolds through the ministerial priesthood. According to John Paul II, for
"a careful rereading of the council's teaching concerning the relationship
between the 'priesthood and the faithful,' which results from [. . .] Baptism
[. . .] and the 'ministerial priesthood,'"[30] it is necessary to affirm that

> the priesthood is not an institution that exists "alongside" the laity, or
> "above" it. The priesthood of bishops and priests, as well as the ministry
> of deacons, is "for" the laity, and precisely for this reason it possesses a
> "ministerial" character, that is to say one "of service." Moreover, it high-
> lights the "baptismal priesthood," the priesthood common to all the faith-
> ful. It highlights this priesthood and at the same time helps it to be realized
> in the sacramental life.[31]

However, to affirm that the baptismal and ministerial priesthood "differ
from one another in essence and not only in degree," but also in their mutual
interaction, it does not seem sufficient to establish the distinction between
them. We must go further to find a satisfactory answer to the content of
that distinction. Here, the "service" of the ministerial priesthood is called
to have a "new and special" participation, which is "specific and authori-

---

the hierarchical priesthood and the common priesthood of the faithful" (*Letter* 1979, no. 4). Also,
"the common priesthood of the whole People of God is linked with *the service of the ministers
of the Eucharist*" (*Letter* 1987, no. 1, emphasis in the original).

30 *Letter* 1990, no. 3.

31 *Letter* 1990, no. 3. This report was widely affirmed after the Second Vatican Council. The pope
had already said in his *Letter* 1979, at no. 4: "This sacrament [of Orders] . . . by virtue of its very
nature and of everything that it produces in our life and activity, serves to make the faithful
aware of their common priesthood and to activate it." He added, "We should understand our
ministerial priesthood as 'subordination' to the common priesthood of all the faithful, of the
laity" (*Letter* 1979, no. 9). Later he will say that "we have likewise become servants of the royal
priesthood of the whole People of God, of all the baptized, so that we may proclaim the *magnalia
Dei*, the 'mighty works of God' (Acts 2:11)" (*Letter* 1993, no. 2). Ultimately, "the priest is for the
laity" (*Letter* 1986, no. 10). *Pastores dabo vobis* also states that "the ordained priesthood ought
not to be thought of as existing prior to the Church, because it is totally at the service of the
Church. Nor should it be considered as posterior to the ecclesial community, as if the Church
could be imagined as already established without this priesthood" (*PDV 16*).
　　It can be concluded that the hierarchical priesthood "does not exist without the common
priesthood because it exists for the common priesthood. The latter, in turn, does not exist without the ministerial priesthood because it exists by virtue of the ministerial priesthood." Agostino
Favale, *Il ministero presbiterale. Aspetti dottrinali, pastorali, spirituali*. (Rome: Pontificio Ateneo
Salesiano, 1989), 127.

tative"[32] to the priesthood of Christ. This is proper participation in "the authority by which Christ builds up, sanctifies and rules his Body,"[33] and this constitutes its particularity and purpose. This could only be done through a deep inner transformation of the one who receives the sacrament of the Orders. The doctrine of "character"[34] is "the basis of our identity,"[35] and thus helps us to deepen the answer already sketched out.

> *The priesthood in which we share through the sacrament of Orders,* which has been forever "imprinted" on our souls through a special sign from God, [. . .] the "character" [that] *remains in explicit relationship with the common priesthood of the faithful.*[36]

32 *PDV* 15, 16.

33 *PO* 2. It could be added "that they can help the People of God to exercise faithfully and fully the common priesthood which it has received" (*PDV* 17). The *CCC*, no. 1547, summarizes: "While the common priesthood of the faithful is exercised by the unfolding of baptismal grace—a life of faith, hope, and charity, a life according to the Spirit—, the ministerial priesthood is at the service of the common priesthood. It is directed at the unfolding of the baptismal grace of all Christians. The ministerial priesthood is a means by which Christ unceasingly builds up and leads his Church. For this reason it is transmitted by its own sacrament, the sacrament of Holy Orders."

34 Cf. *CCC*, no. 1597. The first Father of the Church to develop a systematic teaching on character is Augustine: cf. *Sermo ad Caesarensis ecclesiae plebem*, 2: *PL* 43,691. The doctrine of the character "is one of the firm points of Catholic teaching on the priesthood." Saraiva Martins, *Il sacerdozio ministeriale*, 141. Character is "a configuration and special participation in the priesthood of Christ. It is not purely functional, but ontological and concerns the entire person of the ordained minister. It is different from the character of the Baptismal priesthood, which ontologically transforms the impoverished person from sin because of Adam's fault. By the merits of Christ, [the person] becomes a new being, that is to say, justified. The character of the sacrament of Holy Orders offers and imposes on the baptized a new way of being so that he can effectively represent the work of Christ for the benefit of salvation. [. . .] Sacramental grace [. . .] empowers and ontologically transforms the baptized person by making him [. . .] adapted to represent the action of Christ in the evangelization and sacramental life of the Church as head and pastor. Because of this transformation, the ordained minister becomes an effective instrument and image of Christ, the only mediator of salvation for all mankind, thus becoming *servus Christi—Christ's servant.*" Ettore Malnati, *I ministeri nella Chiesa* (Milan: Paoline, 2008), 154. Saint Augustine describes the notion of character in a functional way as *jus dandi*, a necessary condition for the valid administration of the sacraments. The priest by his own power cannot give what he does not have. However, thanks to the sacramental consecration, it is the Christ Himself who acts by his person: his is the voice which, once emitted, disappears to give place to the action of the Word. Cf. speech of Cardinal Joseph Ratzinger at the Anniversary Congress of *Presbyterorum Ordinis Decree*, October 23–28, 1995, available at http://www.clerus.org/clerus/dati/1998–12/13–6/Ratzinger_symposio.rtf.html. A recent book on this subject: David Toups, *Reclaiming our Priestly Character* (Omaha: IPF Publications, 2008), 31–96.

35 *Letter* 1979, no. 4.

36 *Letter* 1979, no. 3, emphasis in the original. "*[P]riestly service* [is] *a special sharing, though the priestly character of Holy Orders, in [Christ's] own priesthood*" (*Letter* 1991, no. 1, emphasis in the original).

Indeed, on the day of priestly ordination, priests receive a "charism of God" (2 Tim 1:6) and a "spiritual gift" (1 Tim 4:14), and they are "consecrated by God in a new manner."[37] This inaugurates a new way of being because it is a permanent gift of grace, inherent in the person who receives it, which permanently empowers him to act like Christ:[38] "Christ revealed to the Apostles that their vocation was to become priests like him and in him."[39] This particular participation in the priesthood of Christ is a participation not only of acting in favor of men, as a specific mission, but necessarily and above all at the level of the priestly being through consecration.

> [A]ccording to the faith of the Church, priestly ordination not only confers a new mission in the Church, a ministry, but a new *consecration* of the person, one linked to the character imprinted by the sacrament of Orders as a spiritual, indelible sign of a special belonging to Christ in being and, consequently, in acting.[40]

It is for this reason that the pontifical magisterium affirms its "awareness of the specific ontological bond which unites the priesthood to Christ,"[41] and that makes him a "continuation of Christ Himself, the one High Priest of the new and Eternal Covenant, [. . .] a living and transparent image of Christ the priest,"[42] by virtue of the character imprinted

---

37 PO 12.

38 Cf. Pius XI, *Ad catholici sacerdotii* (December 20, 1935). "The sacrament of Orders imprints on the soul of the priest a special character which, once it has been received, remains in him as a *source of sacramental grace*, and of all the gifts and charisms which correspond to the vocation to priestly service in the Church" (*Letter* 1991, no. 3). Cf. also: *Letter* 1990, no. 1; *PDV* 70.

39 *Letter* 1996, no. 4. In his letters, John Paul II often returns to this special and proper participation of priests in the priesthood of Christ: cf. *Letter* 1979, no. 3, 4; *Letter* 1987, no. 1, 7; *Letter* 1991, no. 1, 2; *Letter* 1992, no. 2; *Letter* 1993, no. 3; *Letter* 1996, no. 2, 4; *Letter* 1997, no. 5. Of course, the pope follows conciliar teaching: cf., among others: *LG* 10, 28, 62; *PO* 1, 2, 5, 7, 10, 22.

40 *General Audience*, May 26, 1993. On this subsequent consecration to Baptism and Confirmation, cf. *General Audience* of March 31, 1993; *PDV* 12, 16, 18, 20, 21, 22, and 70. The priest acts as Christ by virtue of a "sacred power," as will be discussed later, received at the time of priestly consecration. The philosophical adage states: *Agere sequitur esse* (action follows being). If the priest acts as Christ, it is because of the profound transformation that takes place in him through ordination.

41 *PDV* 11.

42 *PDV* 12. This is where the specificity of the ordained ministry lies. Indeed, the priest is "memory" of Christ, sacrament of his mediation, as will be seen in chapter 3 of this study. The baptismal priesthood, as previously asserted, has a deep religious meaning and is exercised through the offering of one's own life in charity. The common priesthood of all the faithful (lay people and clergy) is part of the newness of the priesthood of Christ, which is also affirmed (cf.

forever.[43] This definitively expresses and deepens the sense of the ordained ministry in the Christian community as gift and service, by which God Himself "summoned those whom He wanted" (Mk 3:13) among the baptized and is committed to acting forever in favor of men. In other words, the reference of John Paul II to this subject helps us understand that the ministerial priesthood has a Christological-pneumatological[44] source and that its destination can only be ecclesial. Thus, since the priest acts in the role of Christ Himself, the proper grace of the ministerial priesthood is in the order of instrumental means:[45] it is a gift of the Lord and an instrument that allows the accomplishment of the common priesthood, to lead God's people to the perfection of charity.

VOBIS SUM EPISCOPUS, VOBISCUM SACERDOS— FOR YOU I AM A BISHOP, WITH YOU I AM A PRIEST

John Paul II emphasizes, in all his letters addressed to the priests, the close link that unites their ministry to the episcopal ministry.[46] In recalling the Chrism Mass, usually celebrated on the morning of Holy Thursday,[47] he echoes what was already said to them in 1979, using similar expressions, in the letters of the following years.

> [Today is] the annual feast of our priesthood, that unites the whole Presbyterium of each Diocese about its Bishop in the shared celebration of the Eucharist.[48]

---

chap. I.1.): it is accessible to all and makes them capable of free access to God, in the sanctuary ("through the blood of Jesus we have confidence of entrance into the sanctuary," Heb 10:19). Also, all Christians can offer sacrifices that are no longer external but internal, because it is the personal offering of their own lives ("offer your bodies as a living sacrifice, holy and pleasing to God, your spiritual worship," Rom 12:1). In this regard, cf. Albert Vanhoye, *Vivere Nella Nuova Alleanza* (Rome: Edizioni ADP, 1995), 231–43.

43 There is "an indelible link that expresses the total dependence of the minister on Christ, so that everything is truly renewed to Him, even in the absence of personal holiness. This specific and objective connection comes from Christ and necessarily and definitively invests the person of the minister." Testa, *I sacramenti della Chiesa*, 299. Thus, the priest always acts in *persona Christi* even if ipso facto he does not have the sanctity of Christ.

44 This subject will be addressed later.

45 *CCC*, no. 1547: "the ministerial priesthood is a means by which Christ unceasingly builds up and leads his Church."

46 *Vobis sum episcopus, vobiscum sacerdos* comes from the first paragraph heading in Latin of *Letter* 1979. The expression is also taken up in *Letter* 1985, no. 2.

47 *Roman Missal*, p. 190.

48 *Letter* 1979, no. 1.

It also gives the main reason for this annual gathering around the pastor of the local church, in "priestly assemblies":[49]

> On this day the priests of the whole world are invited to concelebrate the Eucharist with their bishops and with them to renew the promises of their priestly commitment to the service of Christ and his Church.[50]

In other words, he will say: "We gather, within our various priestly communities, around our bishops, in order to rekindle the sacramental grace of Orders,"[51] "*grace given to you* 'through the laying on of the hands' (cf. 2 Tm 1:6)."[52]

Therefore, these "priestly assemblies" are the place to demonstrate deep priestly unity as well as the differentiation between the episcopate and the presbyterate. These two principles of unity and distinction delimit the identity of the priest. I hope to deepen these themes while initially clarifying the issue at hand: "the annual feast of our priesthood."

Dies natalis sacerdotii—The Birth of the Priesthood

Above all, one must dwell on the question of the institution of the ministerial priesthood itself. This priesthood, "new, visible and external,"[53] distinct from the baptismal priesthood by its essence, was born—according to the words of the pope—on the first Holy Thursday when Christ instituted the Eucharist.

> And therefore, though the dates of our ordination differ, Holy Thursday remains each year the birth of our ministerial priesthood.[54]

---

49 *Letter* 1982, no. 1.

50 *Letter* 1986, no. 1.

51 *Letter* 1990, no. 2.

52 *Letter* 1987, no. 1, emphasis in the original.

53 Ecumenical Council of Trent, *Doctrina et canones de sacramento ordinis* (*Sessio* XXIII, July 15, 1563), chap. 1: *DS* 1764. Here one finds the perspective reported at length in chapter 1, concerning the Letter to the Hebrews.

54 *Letter* 1983, no. 1. He will also say that the Eucharist "is the principal and central *raison d'être* of the sacrament of the priesthood, which effectively came into being at the moment of the institution of the Eucharist, and together with it." *Letter* 1980, no. 2.

The simplicity of the statement could make us forget the complexity of the question. Can it be said that "Holy Thursday [is] the birth of our ministerial priesthood," as John Paul II has suggested on many occasions?[55]

The *dies natalis apostolici sacerdotii* (birth of the apostolic priesthood), that is to say, the precise moment of priestly consecration of the Apostles, for a long time—and particularly since the twelfth century—has been the subject of controversy and debate.[56] Until this period the ancient Fathers, despite the hesitation of some, find a great consistency when they see the sacerdotal consecration of the Apostles in the gift of the Holy Spirit at either Easter or Pentecost, or both.[57]

The opinion that the Twelve received the grace of the priesthood at the Last Supper goes back to Stephen of Autun and Albert the Great. They based themselves on the theory that the *traditio instrumentorum*[58] determines the essential element[59] of the sacrament of the Holy Orders, and they linked

---

55 *Letters* 1982, no. 1; 1983, no. 1; 1985, no. 1 and no. 8: "In liturgia antiqua, cuius Sacerdotes seniores etiam nunc meminerunt, Missae Sacrificium aperiebatur precatione ad pedem altaris, ubi primae voces Psalmi ita resonabant: 'Introibo ad altare Dei; ad Deum qui laetificat iuventutem meam'" (here, the note which accompanies the quotation is this: Ps. 43[42], 4 [Vulg.]; cf. Ambrosius, *Expositio Evang. sec. Lucam* VIII,73: "Pulchre mihi hodie legitur legis exordium, quando mei *natalis est sacerdotii* ; quotannis enim quasi de integro videtur incipere sacerdotium, quando temporum renovatur aetate"; cf. Ecumenical Council of Trent, sess. XXIII, CI, *De institutione sacerdotii Novae Legis*); 1986, conclusion; 1987, no. 1; 1989, no. 2 and no. 3; 1998, no. 7; 2002, no. 11.

56 Erio Castelluci, *Il ministero ordinato* (Brescia: Queriniana, 2002), 154–55.

57 I refer again to the study of Joseph Lecuyer, who quotes several Fathers and ecclesiastical authors: *Il sacerdozio di Cristo e della Chiesa* (Bologna: Dehoniane, 1965), 279–96. There are three different positions: some say that the Twelve were consecrated on Easter day (cf. Jn 20:19–23), such as Origen, John Chrysostom, Ammonius of Alexandria, and Hesychius of Jerusalem; others see the day of their consecration at Pentecost (cf. Acts 2:1–4), such as Irenæus, Hippolytus of Rome, Athanasius, and Severin of Gabala (in Syria); others speak of a double sacerdotal unction (Easter and Pentecost, the latter perfecting the first), like Gregory Nazianzen, Cyril of Jerusalem, Cyril of Alexandria, Pseudo-Dionysius, James of Sarug (Syria), Maximus the Confessor, and Germanus of Constantinople, but also Middle Eastern theologians such as Nicolas Cabasilas, Gregory Palamas, and Simeon of Thessalonica, and Latin theologians Peter Damian, Honorius of Autun, Abelard, and Richard of Saint Victor.

58 Or the *porrectio instrumentorum*, that is to say, the handing over of the paten and the chalice with bread and wine for the Sacrifice, during the ordination. It is a gesture of Gallican origin, introduced into the liturgy of ordination in the tenth century. Cf. Saraiva Martins, *Il sacerdozio ministeriale*, 183.

59 Pius XII decided the question by his Apostolic Constitution *Sacramentum Ordinis*, of November 30, 1947. He states, at no. 4, that "the *traditio instrumentorum* is not necessary for the validity of the Sacred Orders of the Diaconate, the Priesthood, and the Episcopacy" (*DS* 3859). The *traditio instrumentorum* is no longer to be considered as the subject of the sacrament of the Holy Orders. Therefore, already Pius XII binds Holy Thursday more to the laying on of hands

this gesture to the Lord's Supper. At the Council of Trent, although the *Doctrina et Canones de Sacramento Ordinis* says nothing about it, the *Doctrina et Canones de Missae sacrificio* (September 17, 1562) states: "In the Last Supper [Christ] constituted [the Apostles] priests of the New Testament;"[60] also "if any one shall say, that by those words: 'Do this in remembrance of me,' Christ did not institute the Apostles priests [. . .] let him be anathema."[61]

John Paul II seems to integrate into his own magisterium the Tridentine conciliar teaching, in light of the indications just mentioned. Indeed, from 1982, on the occasion of the annual *Letter to Priests written on the occasion of Holy Thursday*, he speaks of the day of the Lord's Supper as the *dies natalis sacerdotii*. Moreover, when he speaks of the Last Supper as the moment of *"the institution of the Sacrament of the Priesthood and that of the Eucharist*,"[62] he makes it understood that the words of Jesus to his Apostles (cf. Lk 22:19, 1 Cor 11:25) are their own consecration: "By entrusting to the Apostles the memorial of his sacrifice, Christ made them sharers in his priesthood."[63] Finally, "[i]n saying 'Do this,' he refers not only to the action, but also the one called to act; in other words, he institutes the ministerial priesthood, which thus becomes one of the essential elements of the Church."[64]

However, the thought of the pope is open to both theories mentioned, because it presents complementary evidence about the consecration of the Apostles. In fact, John Paul II also incorporates the gift of the Holy Spirit on Easter evening as the moment of priestly ordination for the Twelve.

> On the day of our priestly ordination, by virtue of a unique outpouring of the Paraclete, the Risen One accomplished again in each of us what he accomplished in his disciples on the evening of Easter, and set us in the world as those who continue his mission (cf. Jn 20:21–23). This gift of the Spirit, with its mysterious sanctifying power, is the source and root

---

and the invocation of the gift of the Holy Spirit, in a more paschal and Johannine perspective. Cf. Saraiva Martins, *Il sacerdozio ministeriale*, 184; Castellucci, *Il ministero ordinato*, 203.

60 Ecumenical Council of Trent, *De ss. Missae sacrificio* (November 17, 1562), sess. XXII, chap. 1.

61 Ecumenical Council of Trent, *De ss. Missae sacrificio* (November 17, 1562), sess. XXII, can. 2. On the question, dealt with at this council, of the "moment" when the Apostles received the gift of the priesthood, I refer to the study of Lecuyer, *Il sacerdozio di Cristo*, 276–83. The *CCC*, at no. 611 and no. 1337, resumes these conciliar canons.

62 *Letter 1994*, no. 1, emphasis in the original.

63 *Letter 1996*, no. 4.

64 *Letter 2000*, no. 10.

of the special task of evangelization and of sanctification which is entrusted to us.[65]

Also, during a general audience, the pope spoke about the gift of the Paschal Spirit by saying: "To fulfill this mission the Apostles received, in addition to authority, the *special gift of the Holy Spirit* (cf. Jn 20:21–22), which was manifested at Pentecost as Jesus had promised (Acts 1:8)."[66] These words refer us to the Council, which says the Apostles "were fully confirmed [in this mission] on the day of Pesntecost (cf. Acts 2:1–36) in accordance with the Lord's promise: 'You shall receive power when the Holy Spirit comes upon you, and you shall be witnesses for me in Jerusalem, and in all Judea and in Samaria, and even to the very ends of the earth' (Acts 1:8)."[67]

This indetermination from the pontifical magisterium does not seem to fall into doctrinal uncertainty, but rather manifests the dogmatic richness of the ministerial priesthood. It can be understood that the source—among the Apostles and among those who share this same priesthood—is in this double reference to Christ and the Spirit: Christ realizes it, and the Spirit animates it and makes it universal.[68] This avoids two pitfalls: the Christological dimension giving way to an institutional determinism that may be too juridical, and the pneumatological dimension falling into a spiritualism detached from human reality.[69]

Vos nostri estis fratres—You Are My Brothers

On communion or priestly unity, mentioned above, John Paul II is very clear:

---

65 *Letter* 1998, Introduction.

66 *General Audience*, July 1, 1992, no. 6, emphasis in the original.

67 *LG* 19.

68 John Paul II is thus in perfect harmony with the conciliar magisterium, especially *LG* 28 and *PO* 2. Indeed, "Vatican II, although it does not deny the importance of the Last Supper in the theology of the ministry, treats its institution by no longer referring to a single episode [. . .], but to the global mission [. . .] that the Lord entrusted to the Apostles [. . .]. Institution and mission are thus perfectly united: it is in the entire apostolic mission received from Jesus, before and after Easter, that we can identify the institution of the ordained ministry." Castellucci, *Il ministero ordinato*, 238.

69 Saint Thomas Aquinas, seeking to unify the thought of the Fathers as well as Albert the Great, says that "the Apostles received the power of order before the Ascension, where it is said 'Receive the Holy Spirit" (cf. IV Sent., d. 24, q. 1, a. 2, qc 4, sed contra). A little further on, he affirms that the sacerdotal power was given mainly (*ad principalem actum*) to the Lord's Supper with the words "Do this . . ." and secondly (*ad actum secundarium*) after the Resurrection (cf. IV Sent., d. 24, q. 2, a. 3, ad II).

By virtue of the sacrament of Orders, which I also received from the hands of my Bishop (the Metropolitan of Cracow, Cardinal Adam Stephen Sapieha, of unforgettable memory), you are my brothers.[70]

There is, between bishops and priests, "a special communion of sacrament and ministry," whereby "we all share [. . .] in the very heart of the mystery of Jesus Christ."[71] It is for this reason that "the Second Vatican Council [. . .] so explicitly highlighted the collegiality of the Episcopate in the Church, [and] also gave a new form to the life of the priestly communities, joined together by a special bond of brotherhood, and united to the Bishop of the respective local Church."[72]

The pope uses a strong statement in which he seems to summarize this special communion: "On this holy day, each one of us, as priest of the New Covenant, was born into the priesthood of the Apostles,"[73] and we have "received the apostolic task in the different grades of the Sacrament of Orders."[74] From then on, the sacramental priesthood is apostolic:

> When [Jesus] says to the Apostles: "Do this in remembrance of me!" (Lk 22:19; cf. 1 Cor 11:24f) he constitutes *the ministers of this sacrament* in the Church, in which for all time the sacrifice offered by Him for the redemption of the world must continue, be renewed and be actuated [. . .]. All this, dear brothers, through the apostolic succession is granted to us in the Church.[75]
> By virtue of the apostolic succession begun in the Upper Room [we] celebrate the sacrament of Christ's sacrifice.[76]

And he adds that "this priesthood—ministerial and hierarchical—is shared by us. We received it on the day of our ordination through the ministry of the Bishop, who transmitted to each one of us the sacrament begun with the Apostles—begun at the Last Supper, in the Upper Room, on Holy Thursday."[77] These remarks are a little surprising, because they suggest that

70 *Letter* 1979, no. 1.
71 *Letter* 1979, no. 1.
72 *Letter* 1979, no. 1.
73 *Letter* 1983, no. 1.
74 *Letter* 2001, no. 7.
75 *Letter* 1985, no. 1.
76 *Letter* 1988, no. 2.
77 *Letter* 1983, no. 1.

priests and bishops seem to enjoy an equal succession to the priesthood received by the Apostles. What is this in actuality?

It is known that the question of the relationship between the episcopate and the presbyterate "constitutes the classic cross of theologians."[78] The issues it raises, dogmatically, do not seem to be resolved.[79] Moreover, the Second Vatican Council largely presented the dimensions of the episcopate, without clearly treating the distinction of the two degrees of the priesthood in the sacred order.[80]

This Council affirms, for example, that priests, consecrated by God through the ministry of the bishop, share "by special title in the priesthood of Christ,"[81] and "are united with the bishops in sacerdotal dignity. By the power of the sacrament of Orders, in the image of Christ the eternal high Priest, they are consecrated [. . .] true priests of the New Testament."[82] *Presbyterorum ordinis* continues in this same line of thought, saying that "all priests, in union with bishops, so share in one and the same priesthood and ministry of Christ."[83] This is why there is a real ontological communion between the priests and the bishops,[84] and it would seem foolish to assert that priests participate less than the bishops in the priesthood of Christ.[85]

Thus, the statements of John Paul II demonstrate a perfect continuity of thought with the teaching of the Council:

> To the gift of this singular presence [in the Eucharist], which brings him to us in his supreme sacrifice and makes him our bread, Jesus, in the Upper Room, associated *a specific duty of the Apostles and their successors.* From that time on, to be an apostle of Christ, as are the Bishops and the priests sharing in their mission, has involved being able to act *in persona Christi Capitis.*[86]

---

78 Hubert Müller, "*De differentia inter episcopatum et presbyteratum iuxta doctrina Concilii Vaticani II,*" *Periodica* 59 (1970): 599.

79 Müller, "De differentia inter episcopatum et presbyteratum," 599–618.

80 Müller, "De differentia inter episcopatum et presbyteratum," 600.

81 *PO* 5.

82 *LG* 28.

83 *PO* 7.

84 Saraiva Martins, *Il sacerdozio ministeriale*, 196. Cf. also pages 193–98.

85 According to *LG* 28, "the priest is assigned the same triple ministry [of proclamation, celebration, and pastoral guidance] entrusted to the Bishop." Castellucci, *Il ministero ordinato*, 210.

86 *Letter* 2002, no. 1, emphasis in the original.

Undoubtedly, there is only one source of the priestly ministry, which has the same meaning and pursues the same goals, since it is rooted in the same sacrament of the Order.[87] However, this conciliar affirmation that resonates with the pope leaves an open question: if there is such a unity between the presbyterate and the episcopate, if both participate in the unique priesthood of Christ, how are they precisely distinguished as two distinct sacerdotal degrees in the sacrament of the Order?[88]

Vobis sum episcopus—For You I Am a Bishop

Pope John Paul II seems to highlight an important element of distinction between the presbyteral order and the episcopal order.[89]

> Holy Thursday is every year *the day of the birth of the Eucharist* and *the birthday of our priesthood*, which is above all ministerial and at the same time hierarchical. It is ministerial, because by virtue of Holy Orders we perform in the Church that service which is given only to priests to perform, first of all *the service of the Eucharist*. It is also hierarchical, because this service enables us, by serving, to guide pastorally the individual *communities* of the People of God, in communion with Bishops, who have inherited from the Apostles the pastoral power and charism in the Church.[90]

Then, more briefly, he states: "In fact, you, in union with your Bishops, are the pastors of the parishes and of the other communities of the People of God in all parts of the world."[91]

John Paul II rightly says that our priesthood "is ministerial, because by virtue of Holy Orders we perform in the Church that service which is given only to priests to perform." In reality, both priests and bishops can perform all the priestly service that "is given only to priests to perform." To use the

---

87 *PDV* 74. "The priesthood of priests does not derive from the fullness of the episcopal priesthood, but only from Christ." Saraiva Martins, *Il sacerdozio ministeriale*, 193. Cf. also Martins, 197.

88 For a brief distinction in the history of Christianity between "bishop" and "presbyter," cf. Malnati, *I ministeri nella Chiesa*, 122–29.

89 John Paul II, in his first *Letter to Priests*, in 1979, immediately said: "*Vobis sum Episcopus, vobiscum sum Sacerdos.*" He paraphrases a consecrated expression of Saint Augustine: *Vobis enim sum episcopus; vobiscum sum christianus*—"For you I am a bishop, with you I am a Christian" (*Serm* 340,1: *PL* 38,1483).

90 *Letter* 1985, no. 1, emphasis in the original.

91 *Letter* 1983, no. 4.

words of Saint John Chrysostom: "There is not much difference between priests and bishops."[92] Let us clarify these words.

It should be remembered that priests, as well as bishops, can administer all the sacraments. As ordinary ministers, they administer Baptism, Eucharist, Penance, Matrimony and the Anointing of the Sick. By virtue of presbyteral ordination alone, the minister could not validly administer the sacraments of Confirmation and Holy Orders. However, the priest may be the extraordinary minister of the sacrament of Confirmation, by law or by a particular legal act from the competent authority. Thus, he is authorized to exercise the power of sacramental sanctification received at ordination.[93] He is granted the faculty, not the power as such, which he possesses by his ordination.[94]

Concerning the sacrament of Holy Orders, one must take into account the history of the Church. It is known that some popes granted priests the privilege of administering the sacred order of the diaconate and the presbyterate.[95] In addition, the 1917 *Codex Iuris Canonici*, in force until 1983, asserted that the "Ordinary Minister" of ordination was the bishop and recognized the priest as "extraordinary minister."[96] It can be concluded that

---

92 *"Non multum spatii est inter presbyteros et episcopos."* And he adds that the bishops *"sola namque ordinatione superiores sunt, et hinc tantum videntur presbyteris praestare"* (*In Epistulam I ad Timotheum*, hom., XI,1: *PG* 62,553). They "are superior only for the power to ordain and only for that they are considered greater than the priests."

93 Cf. *Code of Canon Law* cc. 882, 883.

94 "Therefore, the difference between the episcopate and the presbyterate in relation to the administration of Confirmation does not consist in the sacramental power as such, but in its possibility of exercise." Müller, "De differentia inter episcopatum et presbyteratum," 610. Cf. also pages 607–10; Jean Galot, *Theology of the Priesthood* (San Francisco: Ignatius Press, 1984), 179–80. It is therefore a canonical question more than a divine disposition. Moreover, in the Eastern tradition, the priest validly administers the Chrismation of Holy Myron as ordinary minister, like the bishop, by virtue of the sacramental power received at Ordination. For this, cf. cc. 694 and 696 of the *Codex Canonicorum Ecclesiarum Orientalium*. See also D. Salachas, *Teologia e disciplina dei sacramenti nei codici latino e orientale* (Bologna: Edizioni Dehoniane, 1999), 115–22. Trent claimed that the bishop is the "ordinary minister of Holy Confirmation" (*De sacramentis*, March 3, 1547, sess. VII, can. 3), while the Second Vatican Council calls him "original minister" (*LG* 26) to safeguard Eastern discipline. The new *Codex Iuris Canonici* favors Tridentine terminology (cf. c. 882).

95 In the fifteenth century, for example, Boniface IX (cf. Bull *Sacrae religionis*, February 1, 1400), Martin V (cf. Bull *Gerentes ad vos*, November 16, 1427), and Innocent VIII (cf. Bull *Exposcit tuae devotionis*, April 9, 1489) granted this privilege to Abbot Fathers. Without forgetting, well before, that this practice was reported and approved at the Council of Ancyra, in 314, canon 13; John Cassian alludes to it in the fifth century; and that in the eighth century, in Germany, Willehad and Ludgere ordained priests before being themselves bishops.

96 Canon 951. The current *Codex* simplifies things by saying, in canon 1012, "The minister of sacred ordination is a consecrated Bishop."

"the indult of the Roman Pontiff does not give priests sacred power as such, but posits the legal element so that the power conferred by priestly ordination can be validly exercised also with regard to the administration of the sacrament of the Holy Orders."[97] Episcopal consecration is the "sole priestly function reserved exclusively for the Bishop"[98] because "it pertains to the bishops to admit newly elected members into the Episcopal body by means of the sacrament of Orders."[99]

This grace to admit new members to the College of Bishops, presided over by Peter, can be established as the sacramental grace specific to the episcopate. On the other hand, those who receive the episcopal consecration "inherited from the Apostles the pastoral power and charism in the Church."[100] In this way, the episcopal order confers a properly apostolic and exclusive prerogative,[101] given the new character that is permanently acquired and which implies a new mode of being: through him one becomes a member of the *collegium episcoporum* (episcopal college),[102] which succeeds the college of the Apostles, and one receives the pastoral

97 Müller, "De differentia inter episcopatum et presbyteratum," 612. It could be said that the priest has the power, although bound, to confer the diaconal and presbyteral order. However, this faculty can only validly be exercised by concession of supreme authority. Cf. Antonio Piolanti, *I sacramenti* (Vatican City: Libreria Editrice Vaticana, 1990), 488; Galot, *Theology of the Priesthood*, 179–80.

98 Müller, "De differentia inter episcopatum et presbyteratum," 612.

99 *LG* 21. The *Schema de Ecclesia*, 1964, said "it belongs only to Bishops." But the Council did not consider it appropriate to indicate with certainty this prerogative as exclusive of the bishops, taking into account three historical testimonies that attribute to priests the consecration of the patriarch in the Alexandrian Church of the first centuries (precisely until the year 264). Cf. Rahner, *La gerarchia nella Chiesa*, 31. Müller concludes that "materially the Council does not explain the theological difference between the episcopate and the presbyterate, nor does it wish to enter into this discussion." Müller, "De differentia inter episcopatum et presbyteratum," 617.

100 *Letter* 1985, no. 1.

101 The *Directory for the Pastoral Ministry of Bishops*, no. 50, in 1973 emphasized that the bishop is the "apostolic man."

102 "In virtue of sacramental consecration and hierarchical communion with the head and members of the body" (*LG* 22). Lived in *hierarchica communio* (hierarchical communion), the episcopal collegiality strongly affirmed during the Council, which took into account the permanent testimony of Tradition, is an effect of episcopal consecration of great ecclesiological value. Cf. Saraiva Martins, *Il sacerdozio ministeriale*, 190–92. The notion of *collegium episcoporum*, implicit in the New Testament writings, was introduced, as is known, by Clement of Rome and elaborated by Irenaeus of Lyons. "Collegiality [is] the central idea of the conciliar doctrine on the episcopate." Castellucci, *Il ministero ordinato*, 216. Thus, the text of *LG* 22 affirms that it has "two roots of collegiality: the first is of sacramental order and the second one of legal type," by *missio canonica*. Castellucci, *Il ministero ordinato*, 217. Cf. also pages 219–22.

charge of the people of God[103] by the "high priesthood."[104] By his statements mentioned at the beginning of this chapter and here again, John Paul II gives a clean and exclusive element of the episcopate that distinguishes it from the presbyterate.[105]

POTESTAS SACRA (SACRED POWER) FOR SERVICE
. . . potestatem Eucharistiae celebrandae—
Power to Celebrate the Eucharist

John Paul II takes up the traditional teaching, proclaimed at the Council of Trent and resumed at the Second Vatican Council, regarding the "sacred power":[106]

---

103 In the canonical tradition, only those who, in the pastoral practice of the *munus regendi* (mission to govern), have the legislative, executive, and judicial powers are considered "pastors" in the strict sense. Bishops, unlike priests, have these three powers and are pastors of the local church. It is noted that the *Codex* thus integrates theological reflection. John Paul II seems to emphasize this aspect because, he says, "the bishops [. . .] inherited from the Apostles the pastoral power and charism in the Church" (*Letter* 1985, no. 1). The Council already said: "The Sacred Council teaches that bishops by divine institution have succeeded to the place of the apostles, as shepherds of the Church" (*LG* 20). *Cum Petro* and *Sub Petro* (with and under Peter) bishops exercise supreme power in the Church (cf. *LG* 22). The bishops have the pastoral power over the Mystical Body of Christ to ordain the Church, according to the teaching of Thomas Aquinas. Cf. Ignacio Andereggen, *Sacerdocio y Plenitud de Vida* (Buenos Aires: Pontifícia Universidad Católica de Argentina, 2004), 106–11. The priests participate in it, as the Council deepens.

104 *LG* 21. The *primatus sacerdotii*, in the words of Hippolytus of Rome (*Traditio Apostolica*, 3; cf. *Catechism of the Catholic Church*, no. 1586). Cf. also the Pontifical of the Episcopal Ordination, the consecration prayer, which says: "Grant, O Father [. . .] that this, your servant, whom you have chosen for the office of Bishop may shepherd your holy flock. [. . .] May he fulfill before you without reproach the ministry of the High Priesthood." *The Roman Pontifical—The Ordination of a Bishop*, 29. Cf. Saraiva Martins, *Il sacerdozio ministeriale*, 187–90.

105 The episcopate is the fullness of the priesthood since it is the highest degree of participation in the priestly ministry of Christ given to the Apostles and their successors in the full exercise of the *tria munera* (three duties). The bishop is the visible principle of unity in his church, as teacher of the faith, sanctifier, and spiritual guide. Priests collaborate in this function.

106 The *potestas sacra* is a singularly complex subject. Laurent Villemin, in his work *Pouvoir d'ordre et pouvoir de juridiction*, makes a study on the subject which seems quite complete. I refer specifically to pages 323–51 and 395–428. It is essential to keep clear definitions: "The sacramental *munera* (*duties*) are a larger reality than the *potestas* (*power*), whether sacramental or orderly, or hierarchical or jurisdictional. The first power is the capacity to perform strictly sacramental acts; the second is the ability to perform legal acts. [. . .] The two powers have various origins: the first [is of origin] sacramental, the second [is of origin] hierarchical. But the source of both is unique: it is Christ, who acts in the Church either by means of the sacraments or by means of the hierarchical ministry." Gianfranco Ghirlanda, "Episcopato e presbiterato nella *Lumen Gentium*," *Communio* 59 (1981): 67–68. The concept of *potestas sacra*, expressed during the Second Vatican Council, has the advantage of unifying the scholastic notions of power of

The sacrament of Orders [. . .], dear Brothers, [. . .] serves to make the faithful aware of their common priesthood and to activate it: the sacrament reminds them that they are the People of God and enables them "to offer spiritual sacrifices" (cf. 1 Pt 2:5) [. . .]. This takes place, above all, when the priest "by the sacred power that he has in the person of Christ (*in persona Christi*) effects the Eucharistic Sacrifice and offers it to God in the name of all the people" (*LG* 10).[107]

Therefore, the priest enjoys a "sacred power" to offer the Eucharistic sacrifice. This power of which the pope speaks is really a "spiritual power"[108] received from Christ Himself by virtue of sacramental grace.[109] The Apostles "on Holy Thursday received the power to celebrate the Eucharist [. . .]. All of us, therefore . . . receive the same power through priestly Ordination."[110] It is interesting to highlight here that John Paul II brings to the forefront the essential Christological element as a novelty particular to the ministerial priesthood: Christ transmits His priesthood to the Apostles and His successors by ordering them to "do this in memory of me."[111]

The words of the pope, just quoted, implicitly refer to the Tridentine definitions:

---

order and jurisdictional power assumed by the Council of Trent. Following the Second Vatican Council, it seems sensible to affirm that there is only one power, that of Christ, which He gave to the Church so that it may pursue the mission that was entrusted to it: the priest "teaches and rules the priestly people; acting in the person of Christ, he makes present the Eucharistic sacrifice, and offers it to God in the name of all the people" (*LG* 10).

107 *Letter* 1979, no. 4.

108 Cf. *PDV* 21, which says: "By sacramental consecration the priest is configured to Jesus Christ as head and shepherd of the Church, and he is endowed with a "spiritual power" which is a share in the authority with which Jesus Christ guides the Church through his Spirit."

109 In fact, the "sacrament of Holy Orders confers upon the priest sacramental grace which gives him a share [. . .] in Jesus' saving 'power' and 'ministry' [. . .]. At the same time it ensures that the priest can count on all the actual graces he needs, whenever they are necessary and useful for the worthy and perfect exercise of the ministry he has received" (*PDV* 70).

110 *Letter* 1979, no. 11. This is the *potestatem Eucharistiae celebrandae* of the title of this section. In his *Letter* of 1980, the Holy Father will say almost the same thing: the Apostles "received the power to celebrate the Eucharistic sacrifice instituted in the Upper Room on the eve of the passion, as the Church's most holy sacrament, [. . .] the power to make this sacrifice present through the priestly ministry of the Eucharist" (no. 3).

111 1 Cor 11:24–25. This is far from a purely "religious" perspective of the priesthood as a natural institution, which would require, for sacrifice, that there be priests. It is no longer a purely human step but a divine initiative. Castellucci, *Il ministero ordinato*, 175 and 181.

To the Apostles, and to their successors in the priesthood [the Lord gave] the power [that] was delivered of consecrating, offering, and administering His Body and Blood[112] [. . .] and of remitting and retaining sins.[113]

Indeed, "the priest fulfills his principal mission and is manifested in all his fullness when he celebrates the Eucharist."[114] From then on, "the celebrant, as minister of this Sacrifice, is the authentic priest, performing—in virtue of the specific power of sacred ordination—a true sacrificial act that brings creation back to God."[115] Celebrating the Eucharist is the *praecipuum munus* (principal duty), that is to say, that the main mission of the priestly ministry is Eucharistic-sacrificial.[116]

Over and above our commitment to the evangelical mission, our greatest commitment consists in exercising this mysterious power over the body of the Redeemer, and all that is within us should be decisively ordered to this. We should also always remember that to this ministerial power we have been sacramentally consecrated, that we have been chosen from among men "for the good of men" (Heb 5:1). We especially, the priests of the Latin Church, whose ordination rite added in the course of the centuries the custom of anointing the priest's hands, should think about this.[117]

This Eucharistic ordination of the priestly *munus* is voluntarily undeveloped at the Second Vatican Council,[118] although the *Acta Synodalia Con-*

112 Session XXIII, chap. I, July 15, 1563, *Doctrina et Canones de Sacramento Ordinis*: DS 1764.

113 Session XXIII, canon 1, July 15, 1563, *Doctrina et Canones de Sacramento Ordinis*: DS 1771. The Tridentine Fathers do not deny that the ministry of the Word belongs to the priestly ministry. Above all, they wanted to oppose the Protestant doctrines in question. In this regard, cf. Saraiva Martins, *Il sacerdozio ministeriale*, 104–6. Cf. also Castellucci, *Il ministero ordinato*, 172–78.

114 *Letter* 1980, no. 2. The Latin version of this letter says, *Sacerdos munus suum praecipuum implet omnique sua plenitudine se ipse ostendit Eucharistiam celebrando* (cf. *LG* 28, *PO* 2 and 5, *AG* 19).

115 *Letter* 1980, no. 9. As in note 18 above, a hyphen in the official Vatican translation that seems mistaken has been deleted from this quotation.

116 The Doctor Angelicus reminds that the priestly service consists above all of the offering of the Sacrifice: *In sacrificio offerendo potissime sacerdotis consistit officium* (*Summa Theologiae* III, q. 22, a. 4c).

117 *Letter* 1980, no. 11.

118 Castellucci, *Il ministero ordinato*, 231. This orientation does not mean that the "new vision of the ministerial priesthood [. . .] minimizes the meaning of the Eucharistic ministry, but it is a question of placing the priestly ministry in the context of the community leadership service." Maryanne Confoy, *Religious Life and Priesthood* (New York: Paulist Press, 2008), 30.

cilii Oecumenici Vaticani II report the words of the writing committee of *Presbyterorum Ordinis*, recalling that the "Eucharistic *munus* is the fulfillment of the *munus* sacerdotal."[119] Thus, it seems valid to delve into the fact that John Paul II, in his first letter to the priests in 1979 and several times thereafter, returns to "the power to celebrate the Eucharist."[120] Is it a matter of convenience, since these letters are written in the light of the Lord's Supper, which Holy Thursday commemorates, or is this emphasis on the Eucharist intentional such that there is a special significance to this fact beyond the occasion?

The Second Vatican Council vigorously affirms that the "Eucharistic sacrifice [. . .] is the fount and apex of the whole Christian life."[121] The Eucharist is a source for the life of the Church because principally from it "all her power flows" and from it "as from a font, grace is poured forth upon us; and the sanctification of men in Christ and the glorification of God, to which all other activities of the Church are directed as toward their end."[122] The Eucharist is also the summit of the Christian life, because towards it "the activity of the Church is directed."[123]

This being true for every baptized person, the responsibility of the ordained minister is all the more demanding. Chapter II of the Decree *Presbyterorum Ordinis* on the Ministry and Life of Priests deals, among other things, with the "The Ministry of Priests." Having previously mentioned the ministry of the Word of God, the decree states:

> The other sacraments, as well as with every ministry of the Church and every work of the apostolate, are tied together with the Eucharist and are directed toward it. The Most Blessed Eucharist contains the entire spiritual boon of the Church, that is, Christ Himself, our Pasch and Living Bread, by the action of the Holy Spirit through His very flesh vital and vitalizing, giving life to men who are thus invited and encouraged to offer themselves, their labors, and all created things, together with him. [. . .] [T]he Eucharist shows itself as the source and the apex of the whole work of preaching the Gospel. Those under instruction are introduced by stages to a sharing in the Eucharist, and the faithful, already marked with the

119 Expressions from the *Acta* in Castellucci, *Il ministero ordinato*, 231.

120 *Letter 1979*, no. 11.

121 *LG* 11.

122 *SC* 10.

123 *SC* 10.

seal of Baptism and Confirmation, are through the reception of the Eucharist fully joined to the Body of Christ.[124]

Thus, one can conclude that in referring to *Lumen Gentium* 11,[125] John Paul II does not isolate the Eucharistic service of the priestly ministry from its overall ecclesial perspective.[126] Therefore, the link he establishes between the Eucharist and the ministerial priesthood is not a mere convenience linked to the commemoration of Holy Thursday. The pope emphasizes the Eucharistic dimension by referring to it as the dynamic synthesis of the priestly ministry itself:[127]

> From the perpetuation of the sacrifice of the Cross and her communion with the body and blood of Christ in the Eucharist, the Church draws the spiritual power needed to carry out her mission. The Eucharist thus appears as both the *source* and the *summit* of all evangelization, since its goal is the communion of mankind with Christ and in Him with the Father and the Holy Spirit.[128]

The pope expresses himself intensely in his encyclical *Ecclesia de Eucharistia*:

> Every activity aimed at carrying out the Church's mission, every work of pastoral planning, must draw the strength it needs from the Eucharistic mystery and in turn be directed to that mystery as its culmination. In the Eucharist we have Jesus; we have his redemptive Sacrifice; we have his resurrection; we have the gift of the Holy Spirit; we have adoration, obedience, and love of the Father. Were we to disregard the Eucharist, how could we overcome our own deficiency?[129]

---

124 *PO* 5.

125 He quotes this text in several letters: 1980, nos. 2 and 4; 1982, no. 1; 1986, no. 8; 2000, no. 5.

126 It should be pointed out that in the light of *Lumen Gentium* 26, the celebration of the Eucharist is the summit of preaching and the source of unity because "the faithful are gathered together by the preaching of the Gospel of Christ, and the mystery of the Lord's Supper is celebrated, that [. . .] the whole brotherhood may be joined together."

127 The Eucharist "is the principal and central raison d'être of the sacrament of the priesthood." *Letter* 1980, no. 2. Cf. the study of António Couto, *Dom e carisma de ser padre* (Prior Velho: Paulinas, 2008), 100–74.

128 John Paul II, Encyclical *Ecclesia de Eucharistia* on the Eucharist in its relationship to the Church (April 17, 2003), no. 22, emphasis in the original.

129 *Ecclesia de Eucharistia*, no. 60.

For John Paul II, the priestly ministry is integrated into a Eucharistic ecclesiology.[130]

Ministerialem potestatem—Power for Service

For John Paul II the "power to celebrate the Eucharist" signifies a kind of dynamic synthesis of the priestly ministry and the distinctiveness of the sacred power received during ordination,[131] but not, however, from a purely cultic and static conception of the priesthood. Being a synthesis, it refers to a larger dimension, the *ministerialem potestatem*.[132] Certainly, this sacred power is deployed more broadly in the living ecclesial reality of priestly action. One now can discover how the Holy Father presents this aspect.

> *In the Dogmatic Constitution* Lumen Gentium, the Second Vatican Council pointed out *the difference between the common priesthood* of all the baptized and the *priesthood* which we receive in the Sacrament of Orders. The Council calls the latter "ministerial priesthood," which means both "office" and "service." It is also "hierarchical" in the sense of sacred service.[133]

The ministerial priesthood is a sacred service. The *ministerialem potestatem*[134] received by the ordination is oriented towards service, in the image of the act of Christ Himself:[135]

> [T]he question could be put in these terms if the hierarchical priesthood granted a social position of privilege characterized by the exercise of "power." But this is not the case: the ministerial priesthood, in Christ's plan, is an expression not of *domination* but of *service*! Anyone who interpreted it as "domination" would certainly be far from the intention of Christ, who in the Upper Room began the Last Supper by washing the feet of the Apostles. In this way He strongly emphasized the "ministerial" character of the priesthood which He instituted that very evening. "For

---

130 Castellucci, *Il ministero ordinato*, 212 and 214.

131 "The imposition of hands is the sign of the bestowal of the Holy Spirit, who is himself the supreme author of the sacred power of the priesthood: *sacramental and ministerial authority*" (*Letter* 1991, no. 1, emphasis in the original).

132 *Letter* 1980, no. 11. About the priestly ministry as a service, cf. Castellucci, *Il ministero ordinato*, 203–6.

133 *Letter* 1989, no. 2.

134 *Letter* 1980, no. 11.

135 Cf. chapter 1.

the Son of Man came not to be served but to serve, and to give His life as a ransom for many" (Mk 10:45).[136]

In fact, the priestly power entrusted to us by Christ is characterized by "the special care for the salvation of others, for truth, for the love and holiness of the whole People of God, for the spiritual unity of the Church [and] is exercised in various ways."[137] It is a "service of communion."[138] In this same letter he states:

> Of course there is a difference in the ways in which you, dear Brothers, fulfill your priestly vocation. Some in the ordinary pastoral work of Parishes; others in mission lands; still others in the field of activities connected with the teaching, training and education of youth, or working in the various spheres and organizations whereby you assist in the development of social and cultural life; yet others near the suffering, the sick, the neglected, and sometimes, you yourselves bed-ridden and in pain. These ways differ from one another, and it is just impossible to name them all one by one.[139]

In other words, and using conciliar expressions that John Paul II has repeated several times, "the ministerial priest, by the sacred power he enjoys, teaches and rules the priestly people."[140]

> Within all these differences, *you are always and everywhere the bearers of your particular vocation*: you are bearers of the grace of Christ, the eternal Priest, and bearers of the charism of the Good Shepherd. And this you can never forget; this you can never renounce; this you must put into practice at every moment, in every place and in every way. In this consists that "supreme art" to which Jesus Christ has called you. "The supreme art is the direction of souls," wrote Saint Gregory the Great.[141]

---

136 *Letter* 1995, no. 7.

137 *Letter* 1979, no. 6.

138 *CCC*, title of the third chapter "The Sacraments at the Service of Communion," in the second part, second section.

139 *Letter* 1979, no. 6.

140 *LG* 10: "The ministerial priest, by the sacred power he enjoys, teaches and rules the priestly people; acting in the person of Christ, he makes present the Eucharistic sacrifice, and offers it to God in the name of all the people." One can read this text in several *Letters*: 1979, no. 3; 1989, no. 2; 1996, no. 2; 2004, no. 4.

141 *Letter* 1979, no. 6, emphasis in original.

Through the various passages quoted, it is understood that the pope refers to the service of the priestly ministry to the mission that Christ has entrusted to the Church as a whole and to the Apostles in particular. Following the Savior—"good teacher" (Lk 18:18), "high priest" (Heb 7:26), and "pastor" (Jn 10:11–14)—this is the task to evangelize, to sanctify, and to preside in charity,[142] or, quite simply, the task to "prolong throughout history to the end of time the same mission of Jesus on behalf of humanity."[143]

In fact, the priests, being close collaborators of the bishops, successors of the Apostles, also perform the service articulated by the *tria munera*[144] as "teachers for doctrine, priests for sacred worship, and ministers for governing."[145] This means that the sacramental task and the Church's preaching

[142] "The theology of the presbyterate at the Second Vatican Council [. . .] came out of a very dense paragraph of *LG* 28, to a specific decree on the ministry and life of priests, *Presbyterorum Ordinis*, and another on priestly formation, *Optatam Totius*. [. . .] The starting point is no longer the sacerdotal power to consecrate the Eucharist, but the episcopal mission of proclamation, celebration, and pastoral guide shared with the priests." Castellucci, *Il ministero ordinato*, 210. Also, *LG* 18 recalls that the episcopate is a service, and in *LG* 24 the episcopal power aims to be a ministry: "The *potestas* is therefore understood not as a 'command' or a 'dignity,' but rather as 'munus,' 'servitium,' 'diakonia,' 'ministerium.' The fact that this paragraph [*LG* 24] precedes the three successive ones that treat the *tria munera* is decisive: it frames them and gives the exact interpretation, which is diaconal in nature." Castellucci, *Il ministero ordinato*, 223.

[143] *PDV* 14. There are three distinct but interrelated aspects of a single salvific mission. Cf. also *PO* 12 as well as *PDV* 12 and 15. During a priest's ordination, "God takes possession of his personal being to make him a living instrument of his divine action in the world, to enable him to collaborate with him in the realization of his plan of salvation. Therefore, sacerdotal consecration, far from being a separation from the world and from the brothers, implies, on the contrary, a total gift of oneself to the Church and to all humanity." Saraiva Martins, *Il sacerdozio ministeriale*, 170.

[144] On this subject the bibliography is abundant. See especially Yves Congar, "Sur la trilogie: Prophète-Roi-Prêtre," *Revue des Sciences Philosophiques et Théologiques* 67 (1983): 97–115. In the spirit of the Second Vatican Council, the *tria munera* systematize the mission of the Church: this schema is used for the whole Church (cf. *LG* 10–13), evoked for bishops (cf. *LG* 19–21), and extended to priests (cf. *LG* 28 and *PO* 4–6) and laypeople (cf. *LG* 34–36). The common note is the missionary dimension: all the faithful are in charge of announcing salvation.

[145] *LG* 20. *LG* 28 says: "[The priests by] the power of the sacrament of Orders, in the image of Christ the eternal high Priest, are consecrated to preach the Gospel and shepherd the faithful and to celebrate divine worship, so that they are true priests of the New Testament." The Council, "in accordance with its missionary perspective, first names the ministry of the Word: for the Christian life begins with listening to the preached Word. The Eucharistic ministry is presented as the summit because the Eucharist is the summit of the life of the Church. Lastly, the ministry of pastoral guidance is put in relation of subordination with regard to the Bishop." Castellucci, *Il ministero ordinato*, 233. In the *General Audience* of April 21, 1993, no. 2, John Paul II explains why preaching is the priest's first apostolate: "For presbyters, [. . .] *proclaiming of the Word of God is the first task to be carried out*, because the basis of personal and communal Christian life is faith, which results from the Word of God and is nourished on this Word." However, he warns that "any attempt to reduce the priestly ministry to preaching alone or to teaching would

and guidance are rooted in the sacrament of the Holy Orders,[146] because "to this ministerial power we have been sacramentally consecrated, [. . .] we have been chosen from among men for the good of men."[147]

SYNTHESIS

Finally, who is the priest in the mind of Pope John Paul II? Above all, he is a man to whom the Lord has been merciful by regenerating him through the waters of Baptism. He, too, is a child of God, saved from the misguidance of sin. He is a member of a holy and priestly people, called to a holy life, to proclaim the good news of salvation and to guide men who seek to reach God. Undoubtedly, the rehabilitation of the common priesthood of the believers—undertaken by the Council and supported by John Paul II—implies the extension of *missio Christi* (Christ's mission) to the whole Church. The concept of the priesthood is a crucial biblical Christian category applicable to all members of the people of God, who participate in the unique priesthood of Christ.

The priest is a man called from among his brothers. He receives the sacramental anointing that, through an existential transformation, makes him participate in the apostolic priesthood conferred by Christ on the Church; it is in no way a derivation or delegation of the common priesthood. As for Christ—whom the Spirit consecrated in the new priesthood through the events of his Incarnation, Passion, and glorification—this same Spirit consecrates the priest to continue His gestures of salvation. By virtue of the charismatic character, he is at the service of the edification of the community with the authority coming from Christ Himself. Therefore, to be a

---

misunderstand an essential aspect of this ministry. [The sacraments] 'cannot be undervalued, since through them the word is brought to fuller effect, namely communion in the mystery of Christ'" (*General Audience*, May 5, 1993, no. 1, citing the 1971 document of the Synod of Bishops, *Il sacerdozio ministeriale—Messaggio al Popolo di Dio* (November 30, 1971), II.1.a). Finally, "the essential purpose of their activity as pastors and of the authority conferred on them [is to lead] the community entrusted to them to the full development of its spiritual and ecclesial life" (*General Audience*, May 19, 1993, no. 2).

146 In this way, "for the presbyterate [. . .] it is no longer the Holy Orders and the jurisdiction, [the] two sources of the ministry, but only the Holy Orders, from which the ministry derives in its three articulations, regulated by the jurisdiction." Castellucci, *Il ministero ordinato*, 232.

147 *Letter* 1980, no. 11. Indeed, "that duty, which the Lord committed to the shepherds of His people, is a true service" for the edification of the Church (*LG* 24). "This priesthood is ministerial. [. . .] [I]t has been instituted for the good of men and the communion of the Church" (*CCC*, no. 1551).

priest means to be a servant of God and a servant of men, like Christ, who was the servant par excellence, and pursuing His work of sanctification. From then on, the priestly ministry is part of the Christian community and can only be understood in relation to all the people of God. Therefore, there is in the Church a unity of mission and a plurality of ministries (cf. *AA* 2).

In the people of God, the priest is the one who has received a particular gift of grace that enables him, through sacred power, to offer men the goods of salvation. By proclaiming the Kingdom of God and administering the sacraments, the priest centers his life on the salvific action of God in Christ. The apostolic exhortation *Pastores dabo vobis* states that "the relation of the priest to Jesus Christ, and in him to his Church, is found in the very being of the priest by virtue of his sacramental consecration/anointing and in his activity, that is, in his mission or ministry" (*PDV* 16). In a special way, "the priest minister is the servant of Christ present in the Church as mystery, communion, and mission. In virtue of his participation in the 'anointing' and 'mission' of Christ, the priest can continue Christ's prayer, word, sacrifice, and salvific action in the Church."[148] It is a service for communion between men and God and men among themselves. It is above all a service of an ecclesiology of Eucharistic communion, that is, where all the priestly activity converges towards the Eucharist, insofar as it is "the fount and apex of the whole Christian life."[149] Also, having rehabilitated the patristic ecclesiology of communion, the close bond which unites the presbyterate to the episcopate is recovered, and the sacramental unity of these two degrees of the Holy Orders—priestly in nature—is affirmed. If both participate in the apostolic priesthood, the episcopate is the legitimate ecclesial origin of the priestly mission. The Chrism Mass of Holy Thursday is the visible expression of this ecclesiology, where the priestly communion is demonstrated around the Eucharist between the presbyterate and the bishop and between them and all the baptized.

Finally, John Paul II, following the Second Vatican Council—which deepens and completes that of Trent—recalls that the sacrament of Holy Orders establishes a relationship not only with God but also with the Church and the world. The ordained ministry has an ecclesiological char-

---

148 Synod of Bishops, Eighth Ordinary General Assembly, "The Formation of Priests in the Circumstances of the Present Day" (1990), Instrumentum Laboris, 16; cf. Proposition 7, cited in *PDV* 16.

149 *LG* 11.

acter (cf. *PO* 2). The foundations for a more balanced relationship between the Christological and ecclesiological dimensions, as well as the ontological and functional aspects of the ordained ministry, are adequately established and unambiguous. The priest's isolation was ended by establishing links with the common priesthood, the presbyterate, and the sacramentality of the episcopate, and by establishing a more harmonious relationship between the individual and community dimensions of ministry and between worship and apostolate. Thus, having clearly established the identity of the priest, the following chapter treats his own mission in the Church.

Chapter 3

The Priest, "Memory" of Christ

The preceding chapters have enabled us to emphasize the sources used for John Paul II's Holy Thursday letters (chapter 1), which led us to clarify the identity of the ordained minister from among the people of God (chapter 2), the latter being characterized by equal dignity, thanks to Baptism, and by a functional distinction desired by the Savior. In this third chapter, the proper mission of the ordained minister in ecclesial communion, as presented by the pope, will be studied. Since "Jesus Christ has revealed in himself the perfect and definitive features of the priesthood,"[1] the priest, configured to Christ, must manifest in his life his priestly action. Indeed, he is the "memory" of Christ in the world because he is "the one who belongs to God and makes people think about God."[2]

CELIBACY FOR A GREATER GIFT

In his first letter, in 1979, John Paul II addressed the question of priestly celibacy. He returned to and completed his thought with other letters in successive years. Other pontifical texts provide a rather complete vision of the subject. His intention is clear on this subject.

> We can only seek to understand this question [of celibacy] more deeply and to respond to it more maturely, freeing ourselves from the various objections that have always—as happens today too—been raised against priestly celibacy, and also freeing ourselves from the different interpretations that appeal to criteria alien to the Gospel, to Tradition, and to the Church's Magisterium—criteria, we would add, whose "anthropological" correctness and basis in fact are seen to be very dubious and of relative value.[3]

Thus, from these writings, celibacy can be presented in its various Christological, eschatological, ecclesiological, anthropological, and canon-

1 *PDV* 13.

2 *PDV* 47.

3 *Letter* 1979, no. 8.

ical motivations. A sixth reason could be added, which seems to synthesize the whole: the spousal dimension of ecclesiastical celibacy.

The Christological Foundation

An important reason, seldom mentioned in the letters but which justifies priestly celibacy, is Christ Himself. It is He, actually, who exerts such a fascination in the life of the one who lets himself be grasped by His person, who binds us in an "absolute attachment to the person and redeeming work of Christ, with a radical renunciation that can seem confusing to human eyes. Jesus himself, in suggesting it, observed that not everyone can understand it (cf. Mt 19:10–12). Blessed are they who receive the grace to understand it and remain faithful on this journey!"[4] In this way, the "[v]irginal fidelity to the Spouse, which finds its own particular expression in this form of life [of the priestly celibacy], enables us to share in the intimate life of the Church."[5] Thus, this exclusive relationship of the heart and the undivided love for Christ direct the entire capacity to love for the ordained minister. However, the Christological dimension does not only determine this personal relationship to Christ in celibacy. As a matter of fact, the *forma vivendi Christi* appropriately becomes the lifestyle of the one who is its sacramental image:

> Jesus is the concrete ideal of this form of consecrated life, an example for everyone, but especially for priests. He lived as a celibate, and for this reason he was able to devote all his energy to preaching the kingdom of God and to serving people with a heart open to all humanity, as the founder of a new spiritual family. His choice was truly "for the sake of the kingdom of heaven" (cf. Mt 19:12).
>
> By his example Jesus gave an orientation that was followed. According to the Gospels, it appears that the Twelve, destined to be the first to share in his priesthood, renounced family life in order to follow him.[6]

Through the way of life that Christ adopted on earth, He inaugurated and "proposed the *ideal* of celibacy for the new priesthood he was instituting."[7]

---

4 *General Audience*, July 17, 1993, no. 6.

5 *Letter* 1988, no. 5.

6 *General Audience*, July 17, 1993, no. 3.

7 *General Audience*, July 17, 1993, no. 4, emphasis in the original.

The Eschatological Foundation

The eschatological dimension seems to prevail over the other aspects. Indeed, celibacy chosen "for the sake of the kingdom of heaven" is a theme that often comes up in the pope's writings on the subject.

> The Latin Church has wished, and continues to wish, referring to the example of Christ the Lord himself, to the apostolic teaching and to the whole Tradition that is proper to her, *that all those who receive the sacrament of Orders should embrace this renunciation "for the sake of the kingdom of heaven."*[8]

The eschatological dimension is the first scriptural reason which, par excellence, justifies priestly celibacy. For, since "the children of the resurrection neither marry nor take wives,"[9] the "words concerning celibacy for the sake of the kingdom of heaven are coupled with the explanation that Christ offers to the Apostles: 'Not all can receive this saying, but only those to whom it is given' (Mt 19:11)."[10]

Priestly celibacy thus becomes a testimony to the values of the world to come, perceived in the apostolic era as imminent. One understands from the words of the Lord that "it is because of this eschatological perspective that celibacy has meaning and can be chosen."[11] The life of the one who assumes it is a current and permanent sign of the eschatological values of such a kingdom. Celibacy lived "for the sake of the kingdom of heaven" anticipates the highest paschal state of the Christian life. But also,

> in the Gospel according to Matthew, shortly before the passage [. . .] about leaving loved ones, Jesus expresses in strong Semitic language another renunciation required "for sake of the Gospel," that is, the renunciation of marriage: "Some have made themselves eunuchs for the sake of the kingdom of God" (Mt 19:12). They are committed to celibacy, that is, in order to put themselves entirely at the service of the "Gospel of the kingdom" (cf. Mt 4:23; 9:35; 24:34).[12]

---

8 *Letter* 1979, no. 8, emphasis in the original.

9 *PO* 16. This text recalls Mt 22:30, Mk 12:25, and Lk 20:35.

10 *Letter* 1993, reflections. https://www.vatican.va/content/john-paul-ii/fr/letters/1993/documents/hf_jp-ii_let_08041993_priests.html. Accessed July 27, 2021. These reflections are only available with the French version of the text.

11 Thaddée Matura, "Le célibat dans le Nouveau Testament d'après l'exégèse récente," *Nouvelle Revue Théologique* 97 (1975): 602.

12 *General Audience*, July 17, 1993, no. 2.

John Paul II understands priestly celibacy in its privileged relation to the kingdom. However, it is not only perceived from a perspective of an eschatological witness, as has been pointed out before, but also from the perspective of mission, because "the kingdom of God is among you" (Lk 17:21) and one will devote oneself wholly to the service of the kingdom of God. This perception opens us to the ecclesiological dimension of celibacy.

The Ecclesiological Foundation

Concerning the ecclesiological aspect of celibacy, the Holy Father recalls that we "link our priestly vocation to celibacy," that is to say, "'making ourselves eunuchs for the sake of the kingdom of heaven.'"[13] The priest is undeniably called to respond to the gift made to him by God, because "celibacy is a gift for the individual and, in him and through him, a gift for the Church."[14] It is a charism,[15] one given for personal sanctification and for the edification of the whole Church.[16]

In his first *Letter*, in 1979, John Paul II emphasized this dimension of priestly celibacy in a rich and dense comment, which ought to be shared widely.

> [The] celibacy "for the sake of the kingdom" is not only an eschatological sign; it also has a great social meaning, in the present life, for the service of the People of God. Through his celibacy, the Priest becomes the "man for others," in a different way from the man who, by binding himself in conjugal union with a woman, also becomes, as husband and father, a man "for others," especially in the radius of his own family [. . .]. The Priest, by renouncing this fatherhood proper to married men, seeks another fatherhood and, as it were, even another motherhood, recalling the words of the Apostle about the children whom he begets in suffering.
>
> These are children of his spirit, people entrusted to his solicitude by the Good Shepherd. These people are many, more numerous than an ordinary human family can embrace. The pastoral vocation of priests is great, and the Council teaches that it is universal: it is directed towards the whole Church, and therefore it is of a missionary character. Normally, it is linked

---

13 *Letter* 1988, no. 5.

14 *Letter* 1993, reflections.

15 "The Catholic Church [. . .] wishes to remain faithful to the charism which she has received and embraced as a gift from her Lord and Master" (*Letter* 1993, reflections).

16 In *Homily* 1984, no. 4, he says, "Let each one of us basically preserve his gift in all the wealth of its expressions; including the magnificent gift of celibacy voluntarily consecrated to the Lord— and received from him—for our sanctification and for the building up of the Church."

to the service of a particular community of the People of God, in which each individual expects attention, care, and love. The heart of the priest, in order that it may be available for this service, must be free. Celibacy is a sign of a freedom that exists for the sake of service. According to this sign, the hierarchical or "ministerial" priesthood is, according to the tradition of our Church, more strictly "ordered" to the common priesthood of the faithful.[17]

In the pope's thinking, the ecclesiological dimension of celibacy is also a manifestation of an apostolic and missionary availability. Indeed, "the unmarried Christian [. . .] will be able to devote his energies and his time 'to the affairs of the Lord,' that is to say to the new world which already points to the current structures."[18] Celibacy thus becomes "at the same time a sign and a stimulus for pastoral charity and a special source of spiritual fecundity in the world."[19]

The Anthropological Foundation

Referring to the encyclical of Paul VI, *Sacerdotalis caelibatus*, of June 24, 1967,[20] which confronted those "who strongly maintain that priests by reason of their celibacy find themselves in a situation that is not only against nature but also physically and psychologically detrimental to the development of a mature and well-balanced human personality"[21] and that "in the world of our time the observance of celibacy has come to be difficult or even impossible,"[22] John Paul II brings an understanding that

---

17 *Letter* 1979, no. 8. Also, in *Letter* 1988, no. 5, he says: "We freely renounce marriage and establishing our own family, in order to be better able to serve God and neighbor. It can be said that we renounce fatherhood 'according to the flesh,' in order that there may grow and develop in us fatherhood 'according to the Spirit' (cf. Jn 1:13), which, as has already been said, possesses at the same time maternal characteristics."

18 Matura, "Le célibat dans le Nouveau Testament," 496. In his *General Audience* of July 17, 1993, the pope affirms: "In his First Letter to the Corinthians, the apostle Paul states that he had resolved to take this path [of celibacy] and shows the coherence of his own decision, declaring: 'An unmarried man is anxious about the things of the Lord, how he may please the Lord. But a married man is anxious about the things of the world, how he may please his wife, and he is divided' (1 Cor 7:32–34). It is certainly not fitting for someone to be 'divided,' someone who, like the priest, is concerned about the things of the Lord'" (no. 2).

19 *PO* 16.

20 At the Second Vatican Council, Paul VI had found it opportune to ban the Fathers from public discussion of the issue of celibacy and promised a document as a response to expectations. This encyclical is the fruit of the pope's reflection.

21 Paul VI, Encyclical *Sacerdotalis caelibatus* on the celibacy of the priest (June 24, 1967), no. 10.

22 *Sacerdotalis caelibatus*, no. 1.

offers an anthropological answer to the objections of those who oppose sacerdotal celibacy.

> We are all aware that "we have this treasure in earthen vessels" (cf. 2 Cor 4:7); yet we know very well that it is precisely a treasure. [. . .] Celibacy is precisely a "gift of the Spirit." A similar though different gift is contained in the vocation to true and faithful married love, directed towards procreation according to the flesh, in the very lofty context of the sacrament of Matrimony.[23]

Celibacy for the kingdom is thus placed in this perspective of love and self-giving through the body, which concretely expresses the reality of a call.[24] He who is called to conjugal love manifests with his whole being—and including through his body—the love for the other and the openness to life, and in the same way, the one who is called to celibacy for the kingdom also manifests himself in his state of life as a gift to others and for a fruitfulness other than the carnal.[25] Indeed,

> in virginity and celibacy, chastity retains its original meaning, that is, of human sexuality lived as a genuine sign of and precious service to the love of communion and gift of self to others. This meaning is fully found in virginity which makes evident, even in the renunciation of marriage, the "nuptial meaning" of the body through a communion and a personal gift to Jesus Christ and his Church which prefigures and anticipates the perfect and final communion and self-giving of the world to come.[26]

---

23 *Letter* 1979, no. 8. According to John Paul II, priests are men who have embraced the "treasure" of celibacy (cf. *Letter* 1979, 22–23).

24 Cf. Nicole Jeammet, *Le célibat pour Dieu—Regard psychanalytique* (Paris: Cerf, 2009). The author, despite a sometimes functional interpretation of celibacy (cf. pages 51–52), comes to an interesting conclusion: there is a "complementarity of marriage and celibacy, each of which privileges a necessary aspect to a relational correctness. [. . .] Some, in their thirst for a love that initially presents itself to them in an absolute way, will instead privilege the 'sealed source,' the dimension of absence, the desire to be everything to all, so that others will feel more concerned with an intimacy of shared life and the exclusivity of a carnal relationship. But from these choices, the challenge will be exactly the same for all: to learn through the days to love each other. It will be necessary to combine absence and presence, independence and dependence, and an exclusive relationship and openness to others" (63–64).

25 In this way "the priest can be open to every new situation, even the most foreign from an ethnic or cultural standpoint, knowing that he must exercise towards the men and women to whom he is sent a ministry of authentic *spiritual fatherhood*, which gains him 'sons' and 'daughters' in the Lord (1 Thes 2:11; Gal 4:19)" (*Letter* 1995, no. 4, emphasis in the original). The gift of self is "a process of self-transcendence, which is fundamental to the development of the person and to the consolidation of a 'successful' humanity." Stefano Guarinelli, *Il celibato dei preti: perchè sceglierlo ancora?* (Milan: Paoline, 2008), 108.

26 *PDV* 29.

From this point of view, he who has received the gift of celibacy sees it as a serene place of human fulfillment and perfection and the unfolding of his affective capacity in self-giving gift to God and to others. Thus, since this state of life leads to a full human realization, it also becomes a means of personal sanctification. And, without presuming upon his own strength to preserve this priceless gift and to be faithful to the word given, the priest must rely on the strength of the "Holy Spirit, who makes it possible to overcome the spirit of this world, [. . .] all human weaknesses and human strategies. We only need not to lose heart, or to create around this vocation and choice a climate of discouragement."[27] It is necessary that everyone should take care "by keeping special watch over one's feelings and over one's whole conduct."[28]

The Canonical Foundation

"The often widespread view that priestly celibacy in the Catholic Church is an institution imposed by law on those who receive the sacrament of Orders is the result of a misunderstanding, if not of downright bad faith."[29] It is

---

27 *Letter* 1993, reflections. In the *Letter* 1979, no. 9, the Holy Father affirms that there are times "when this keeping one's promise to Christ, made through a conscious and free commitment to celibacy for the whole of one's life, encounters difficulties, is put to the test, or is exposed to temptation—all things that do not spare the priest, any more than they spare any other Christian. At such a moment, the individual must seek support in more fervent prayer. Through prayer, he must find within himself that attitude of humility and sincerity before God and his own conscience; prayer is indeed the source of strength for sustaining what is wavering. Then it is there is born a confidence like the confidence expressed by Saint Paul in the words: 'There is nothing that I cannot master with the help of the One who gives me strength' (Phil 4:13). These truths are confirmed by the experience of many Priests and proved by the reality of life. The acceptance of these truths constitutes the basis of fidelity to the promise made to Christ and the Church, and that promise is at the same time the proof of genuine fidelity to oneself, one's own conscience, and one's own humanity and dignity. One must think of all these things especially at moments of crisis, and not have recourse to a dispensation, understood as an 'administrative intervention,' as though in fact it were not, on the contrary, a matter of a profound question of conscience and a test of humanity. [. . .] God also wishes us all to emerge victorious from such tests, and he gives us adequate help for this." Cf. also *PO* 16.

28 *Letter* 1995, no. 5. This paragraph continues: "If in a relationship with a woman the gift and the choice of celibacy should become endangered, the priest cannot but strive earnestly to remain faithful to his own vocation." A canonist will easily note that the *Code of Canon Law* no longer considers only women as "dangerous" for priestly celibacy: "Clerics are to behave with due prudence towards persons whose company can endanger their obligation to observe continence or give rise to scandal among the faithful" (c. 277, §2). In this canon the vigilance demanded of priests is wider.

29 *Letter* 1979, no. 9. Cf. Christian Cochini, *The Apostolic Origins of Priestly Celibacy* (San Francisco: Ignatius, 1990). This book seems insurmountable by the seriousness of the research. It shows the canonical translation of the evangelical value of priestly celibacy in the first centuries of the Church's history.

through these statements that John Paul II addresses the canonical dimension of priestly celibacy in his first letter to priests. It testifies to the perfect integration of the conciliar teaching on this subject.[30]

Celibacy is a charism and a vocation, to which one responds freely, and "every Christian who receives the sacrament of Orders commits himself to celibacy with full awareness and freedom, after a training lasting a number of years, and after profound reflection and assiduous prayer."[31]

Canonical legislation is but a consequence of this commitment made before God, so that it is validated ecclesiastically and protected appropriately.[32] This discipline is also the result of deepening the close bond of propriety between celibacy and the ordained ministry:[33]

---

30 Cf. Ryszard Szczesny, *La dottrina del Vaticano II sul celibato sacerdotale* (Rome: Pontificia Università Lateranense, 1986). In this doctoral thesis, the author presents in detail the evolution of the drafting of the conciliar decrees *Optatam totius*, no. 10, and *Presbyterorum ordinis*, no. 16. By reading, one realizes that the Fathers gradually moved from a "concept of celibacy presented as a simple disciplinary norm to the concept of celibacy as a sanctifying charism" (Szczesny, 2). Thus there is a shift from a purely legal understanding of the Church's precept to a theological understanding of priestly celibacy, based on the mystery of Christ and his mission.

31 *Letter* 1979, no. 9. This paragraph continues: "He decides upon a life of celibacy only after he has reached a firm conviction that Christ is giving him this 'gift' for the good of the Church and the service of others. Only then does he commit himself to observe celibacy for his entire life." Priestly celibacy is not the "price to pay" or *conditio sine qua non* to be ordained a priest: it is the grateful reception of a gift as well as a choice of the Latin Church for only those who have received, discerned, and responded to this gift.

32 In fact, "it is obvious that such a decision obliges not only by virtue of a law laid down by the Church but also by virtue of personal responsibility. It is a matter here *of keeping one's word to Christ and the Church*. Keeping one's word is, at one and the same time, a duty and a proof of the priest's inner maturity; it is the expression of his personal dignity" (*Letter* 1979, no. 9, emphasis in the original). Thus, the "*vocation to celibacy needs to be consciously protected* [. . .] [i]n particular [. . .] by those priests who, following the discipline in force in the Western Church and so highly esteemed by the Eastern Church, have chosen celibacy for the sake of the Kingdom of God. [. . .] Such a defence would not mean that marriage in itself is something bad, but that for him the path is a different one. For him to abandon that path would be to break the word he has given to God" (*Letter* 1995, no. 5; cf. also *Letter* 1996, no. 5).

33 The Second Vatican Council, in *Presbyterorum ordinis*, no. 16, gives the motives for this discipline of celibacy with the priesthood: "Through virginity, then, or celibacy observed for the Kingdom of Heaven, priests are consecrated to Christ by a new and exceptional reason. They adhere to Him more easily with an undivided heart, they dedicate themselves more freely in Him and through Him to the service of God and men, and they more expeditiously minister to His Kingdom and the work of heavenly regeneration, and thus they are apt to accept, in a broad sense, paternity in Christ. In this way they profess themselves before men as willing to be dedicated to the office committed to them—namely, to commit themselves faithfully to one man and to show themselves as a chaste virgin for Christ and thus to evoke the mysterious marriage established by Christ, and fully to be manifested in the future, in which the Church has Christ as her only Spouse. They give, moreover, a living sign of the world to come, by a faith and charity already made present, in which the children of the resurrection neither marry nor take wives."

Jesus did not promulgate a law, but proposed the *ideal* of celibacy for the new priesthood He was instituting. This ideal was increasingly affirmed in the Church. One can understand that in the first phase of Christianity's spread and development, a large number of priests were married men, chosen and ordained in the wake of Jewish tradition. [. . .] This is a phase in the Church's process of being organized, and, one could say, of testing which discipline of the states of life best corresponds to the ideal and "counsels" taught by the Lord. On the basis of experience and reflection the discipline of celibacy gradually spread to the point of becoming the general practice in the Western Church as a result of canonical legislation. It was not merely the consequence of a juridical and disciplinary fact: it was the growth of the Church's realization of the appropriateness of priestly celibacy not only for historical and practical reasons, but also for those arising from an ever better awareness of the congruence of celibacy and the demands of the priesthood.[34]

These considerations, remarkable for their clarity, allow us to grasp the reason for ecclesiastical legislation on priestly celibacy. "In fact, the Church has considered and still considers that it belongs to the logic of priestly consecration and total belonging to Christ resulting from it, in order consciously to fulfill his mandate of evangelization and the spiritual life."[35] Ultimately, assuming celibacy freely before God and the Church,[36] the priest means to assume an evangelical value protected by an ecclesiastical law.

Cf. also *PDV* 29, 50; *CCC*, no. 1579. The argument of propriety between celibacy and the ordained ministry respects the human and religious value of celibacy and at the same time recognizes that it is not required by the nature of the priesthood. The married Eastern clergy is the convincing indication of the lack of requirement. However, even if celibacy is not ontologically related to the priesthood, it follows that it is not completely foreign or accidental. Indeed, the deep reason for priestly celibacy or its suitability and connection with the priestly ministry is a theological and evangelical fittingness: the person of Christ. Cf. Mario Marini, *Le célibat sacerdotal: forme de vie apostolique* (Condé-sur-Noireau: Le Forum, 2006), 99.

34 *General Audience*, July 17, 1993, no. 4.

35 *General Audience*, July 17, 1993, no. 1.

36 This happens during a rite. For this purpose, canon 1037 prescribes: "An unmarried candidate for the permanent diaconate and a candidate for the presbyterate are not to be admitted to the order of diaconate unless they have assumed the obligation of celibacy in the prescribed rite publicly before God and the Church or have made perpetual vows in a religious institute." This rite, in the US, is planned on the very day of diaconal ordination, after the homily: cf. *The Roman Pontifical of Ordination—Ordination of Deacons*. The bishop questions the candidate for the transitory diaconate: "Those of you who are prepared to embrace the celibate state: do you resolve to keep for ever this commitment as a sign of your dedication to Christ the Lord for the sake of the Kingdom of Heaven, in the service of God and man?" (p. 131).

In persona Christi, Ecclesiae sponsi—In the Person of Christ, Spouse of the Church

The different motivations of priestly celibacy already presented can be summarized as follows: the Christological dimension reveals the minister's love for Christ and the adoption of his lifestyle; the eschatological motive presents it as a sign of the world to come; ecclesiological reason shows the meaning of celibacy in the relation of the priest to the mission of the Church in the world; the anthropological aspect shows celibacy as a gift in the service of love; and ecclesiastical discipline "canonizes" this evangelical value and protects it.

However, it seems important to me to present a final element, of which the letters of John Paul II do not speak explicitly but which finds ample basis in his thought: the nuptial dimension of priestly celibacy. Indeed, this spousal dimension seems to be a suitable answer in finding the distinctiveness of ecclesiastical celibacy. Undoubtedly, all that has been said in this part on the Christological, eschatological, ecclesiological, anthropological, and canonical dimensions can be applied without any difficulty to the consecrated life. That is why it is legitimate to ask the question of whether priestly celibacy has a characteristic of its own.

On this nuptial dimension, John Paul II's post-synodal apostolic exhortation *Pastores dabo vobis* affirms that

> the priest is called to be the living image of Jesus Christ, the spouse of the Church. Of course, he will always remain a member of the community as a believer alongside his other brothers and sisters who have been called by the Spirit, but in virtue of his configuration to Christ, the head and shepherd, the priest stands in this spousal relationship with regard to the community. [. . .] In his spiritual life, therefore, he is called to live out Christ's spousal love toward the Church, his bride. Therefore, the priest's life ought to radiate this spousal character, which demands that he be a witness to Christ's spousal love and thus be capable of loving people with a heart which is new, generous and pure—with genuine self-detachment, with full, constant and faithful dedication.[37]

---

37 *PDV* 22. Cf. Congregation for the Clergy, *Directory on the Ministry and Life of Priests*, (January 31, 1994), 13. Cf. also Laurent Touze, *Célibat sacerdotal et théologie nuptiale de l'ordre* (Rome: Pontificia Università della Santa Croce, 2002). In this work, the author also presents the ambiguities that can bring an understanding of celibacy under the spousal aspect. Does *Pastores dabo vobis* indeed reflect a certain ambiguity—or perhaps a wealth of meaning? If at no. 22 the priest is perceived as "spouse of the Church," at no. 29, he seems to be seen as a sign of the

In the nuptial dimension of ecclesiastical celibacy one can perceive a kind of comprehensive synthesis of other reasons. Moreover, it would be an essential sacramental reason, which would thus determine the specific character of priestly celibacy. Indeed, thanks to priestly ordination, the priest "is called to live out Christ's spousal love toward the Church, his bride." The latter, as Cardinal Cláudio Hummes writes, "being the Spouse of Jesus Christ, wishes to be loved by the total and exclusive manner with which Jesus Christ loved her, as her Head and Spouse."[38] Espousement, therefore, includes a strong Christological dimension.

Likewise, the spousal exclusive love of the priest for the Church-bride predicts and evokes the definitive union of Christ and the Church in the world to come in eschatological times. As a sign of Christ, who gives Himself to the Church, celibacy demonstrates that it is fruitful in its action, thanks to the complete and loving gift of his Bridegroom (ecclesiological dimension). In addition, the nuptial motivation for celibacy reveals the measure of the true and complete love of which a man is capable, following Christ (anthropological dimension).

Is the nuptial dimension of sacerdotal celibacy the essential sacramental reason? I recognize that this represents my own reading of the pope's thought, but in any case, it seems reasonable to me to affirm that the nuptiality qualifies and gathers the reasons of priestly celibacy as properly sacerdotal.[39] Moreover, this spousal relationship—which places the priest "in front of the community"—reveals the profound meaning of his mission: to prepare the Church to meet the true and only Bridegroom, Christ,[40] in the communion of Trinitarian love.

IN PERSONA CHRISTI, PASTOR BONUS—IN THE PERSON OF CHRIST, THE GOOD SHEPHERD

It is now necessary to present the specific mission of the priest. The ordained minister, truly "spouse of the Church," loves her with a total and exclusive

---

nuptiality of the Church with Christ: "Virginity [. . .], even in the renunciation of marriage, [preserves] the 'nuptial meaning' of the body through a communion and a personal gift to Jesus Christ and his Church which prefigures and anticipates the perfect and final communion and self-giving of the world to come."

38 Circular letter from Cardinal Cláudio Hummes, Prefect of the Congregation for the Clergy, April 18, 2009, to the ordinaries, on the new faculties granted by the sovereign pontiff to this dicastery.

39 Touze, *Célibat sacerdotal*, 76.

40 Cf. Eph 5:27; Col 1:22.

love and devotes himself to her. Also, just as ecclesiastical celibacy reveals a deep evangelical value of the priestly mission, this takes on a specific "pastoral" connotation. The priest, like Christ the Good Shepherd (cf. Jn 10: 11–14), leads the Church "to the house of the Lord" (Ps 23:6).

John Paul II used expressions several times that are now familiar to us: the priest is an "other Christ," and through this sacramental representation, he "acts in the role of Christ" as "pastor" of the people of God. Of course, such a quick presentation does not reveal the richness of these statements or their complexity. I propose here to discover their meaning through their use in texts of the Holy Father.

Sacerdos alter Christus—The Priest Is Another Christ

In his letters to priests, John Paul II uses the phrase *Sacerdos alter Christus* only once.[41] He places the priest back in the proper sacramental reality of the ordained ministry and his consecration for service.

> *Sacerdos alter Christus*: This is an expression which indicates how necessary it is that Christ be the starting point for interpreting the reality of the priesthood. Only in this way can we do full justice to the truth about the priest, who, having been "chosen from among men, is appointed to act *on behalf of men in relation to God*" (Heb 5:1). The human dimension of priestly service, in order to be fully authentic, must be rooted in God. Indeed, in every way that this service is "on behalf of men," it is also "in relation to God," that is to say, it serves the manifold richness of this relationship. Without an effort to respond fully to that "anointing with the Spirit of the Lord" which establishes him in the ministerial priesthood, the priest cannot fulfill the expectations that people—the Church and the world—rightly place in him.[42]

One could imagine that this prudent use follows the discretion of the Second Vatican Council, which, for its part, never used it.[43] In addition, the

---

41 The only time John Paul II uses this expression in his Holy Thursday letters is in his *Letter* 1991, no. 2. However, it is found in several other speeches and homilies.

42 *Letter* 1991, no. 2.

43 This was despite the firm request of several Fathers who considered the expression as capable of defining the essence of the ministerial priesthood. The redactors have never given the reasons for this refusal. Cf. Castellucci, *Il ministero ordinato*, 242–43. I do not think that the Council refuses it, but rather integrates this notion into its ecclesiology of communion and mission. Some authors consider this expression ambiguous: cf. C. Wackenheim, E. Schillebeeckx, J. Bunnik, J. Moingt. Others use it without hesitation, clarifying its meaning: cf. J. Galot, J. Saraiva Martins, C. Dillenschneider, A. del Portillo, G. Lemaitre, C. Marmion, P. Socha.

reasons for this omission are unknown and it would be difficult to make assumptions about this. However, it seems appropriate to recall that the expression *alter Christus* is applicable not only to priests but also to all baptized persons (cf. Gal 3:27),[44] as well as to the Church herself, "which here below as another Christ shows forth His person."[45] However, according to John Paul II, as applied to priests, "the expression *Sacerdos alter Christus*, 'the priest is another Christ,' created by the intuition of the Christian people, is not just a way of speaking, a metaphor, but a marvelous, surprising, and consoling reality."[46]

In fact, by deepening what he is, the priest discovers with ever more wonder that his being,[47] conformed to Christ, is the bearer of a grace that surpasses him by its greatness. As a result, he who approaches the ordained minister approaches in a singular way Christ himself and his "ministry." For this reason, it is important to pray "that each priest will attain ever greater maturity in his vocation: in his life and in his service,"[48] so that "[i]n the life of each of us, people should be able to discern the mystery of Christ, the mystery from which originates the reality of the *sacerdos* as *alter Christus*."[49]

By these words, it can be understood that this phrase is not about identifying the priest with Christ as his alter ego. One cannot perceive this expression as a kind of material identification between the two. The phrase *Sacerdos alter Christus* can only be understood to the extent to which it reveals the mission of the ministerial priesthood: deeply and totally assimi-

---

44 "If, as Saint Cyprian said, the Christian is 'another Christ'—*Christianus alter Christus*—with all the more reason it can be said: *Sacerdos alter Christus*." John Paul II, *Gift and Mystery*, 99; cf. also *Speech* to priests at Nepi—Italy (May 1, 1988), no. 2.

45 Pius XII, Encyclical *Mystici Corporis* on the Mystical Body of Christ (June 29, 1943), 77.

46 John Paul II, *Homily* of Priestly Ordination in Rio de Janeiro (July 2, 1980), no. 4. The pope thus seems to want to elucidate the difficult origin of this expression, which is not found as such in the patristic period. That is why, according to the Holy Father, it finds its origin in popular intuition. This understanding of the ordained ministry has found an excellent place of development in the *École Française*.

47 The phrase *Sacerdos alter Christus* first and foremost reveals an ontological reality, which has already been discussed at length elsewhere. Here I emphasize only the consequence of this reality, that is to say, the priestly function of the minister. This is also valid for the other appellations that will be studied afterwards: it is because the priest is configured to Christ that he can act in his name and fulfill the mission that the Lord confides to him.

48 *Letter* 1991, no. 2. He continues, "This maturity contributes in a special way to an increase of vocations. We simply need to love our priesthood, to give ourselves completely to it, so that *the truth about the ministerial priesthood may thus become attractive to others*." Emphasis in the original.

49 *Letter* 1991, no. 2.

lated to Christ, the priest cooperates with all his humanity in his unique priesthood, which makes him an instrument and a sign of His presence in the world.[50] Through him the priesthood of Christ is exercised in sacramental form.[51] This is realized by virtue of the ever-present action that comes solely from Christ and not from a perfect and original personal action of the priest. Thus, the sacramental action of one is the salvific action of the other:[52] the priest is a sacramental Christ.[53]

In persona Christi—In the Person of Christ

When he approaches the priestly mission, John Paul II makes much more use of the expression, which affirms that the priest acts *in persona Christi*:[54]

> Let us open our eyes ever wider—the eyes of our soul—in order to understand better what it means to act *in persona Christi*, in the name of Christ: to act with His power, with the power which, in a word, is rooted in the salvific ground of redemption.[55]

This formulation is old and is found with the Apostle Paul, who affirms to forgive *in persona Christi* (2 Cor 2:10). It would seem that it was introduced into theology by Prosper of Aquitaine.[56] Saint Thomas Aquinas also made use of it and, finally, the ecclesiastical Magisterium adopted the expression at the Council of Florence. The Catechism of the Council of Trent takes up this terminology in the second part, devoted to the sacra-

---

50 Cf. *CCC*, no. 1581: "This sacrament configures the recipient to Christ by a special grace of the Holy Spirit, so that he may serve as Christ's instrument for his Church. By ordination one is enabled to act as a representative of Christ, Head of the Church." Here the instrumentality of the ordained minister is emphasized. And also *CCC*, no. 1584: it is "Christ who acts and effects salvation through the ordained minister."

51 Paul VI said in his *Homily of Priestly Ordination* in the Philippines on November 28, 1970: "Remember that you are 'through Him, with Him and in Him'; each one of you is 'another Christ.'"

52 Cf. *LG* 21; *PO* 2 and 3.

53 This expression joins the title given to this third chapter: the priest is "memory" of Christ, in the sense that he makes his mediation on behalf of men, which has already been stated in the first chapter.

54 *Letters* 1979, 1980, 1984, 1985, 1988, 1989, 1991, 1994, 1995, 1996, 1997, 2000, 2002, 2004, 2005. It can be noted that in *Letters* 1986, no. 10; 1997, no. 5; and 2002, no. 1, John Paul II also uses the expression *in persona Christi Capitis*. This will be approached a little later, when I will speak about the figure of the Good Shepherd.

55 *Homily* 1984, no. 4.

56 Cf. *Psalmorum expositio*, 131: *PL* 51,381. Prosper (circa 390–463) was a close friend and disciple of Augustine.

ments.[57] And, more recently, Vatican Council II does not hesitate to use it in various documents.[58]

The Holy Father, following Tradition, uses this expression especially when it comes to the Eucharistic celebration. In his *Letter* 1980, he gives it an authoritative interpretation that deepens what was just said about the sacramental act of the priest.

> The priest offers the Holy Sacrifice *in persona Christi*; this means more than offering "in the name of" or "in place of" Christ. *In persona* means in specific sacramental identification with "the eternal High Priest" (Opening Prayer of the Second Votive Mass of the Holy Eucharist: Missale Romanum, p. 858) who is the author and principal subject of this sacrifice of His, a sacrifice in which, in truth, nobody can take His place. Only He—only Christ—was able and is always able to be the true and effective "expiation for our sins and . . . for the sins of the whole world" (1 Jn. 2:2). Only His sacrifice—and no one else's—was able and is able to have a "propitiatory power" before God, the Trinity, and the transcendent holiness. Awareness of this reality throws a certain light on the character and significance of the priest celebrant who, by confecting the Holy Sacrifice and acting *in persona Christi*, is sacramentally [. . .] brought into that most profound sacredness, and made part of it, spiritually linking with it, in turn, all those participating in the eucharistic assembly.[59]

By "*the ministers of this sacrament* in the Church, [. . .]" the sacrifice offered by [Jesus] for the redemption of the world must continue, be renewed and be actuated; and He commands these same ministers to act—by virtue of their sacramental priesthood—in His place: *in persona Christi*."[60] But not only during the celebration of this sacrament, because "as at the altar where he celebrates the Eucharist and just as in each one of the sacraments, so the priest, as the minister of penance, acts *in persona*

---

57 Catechism of the Council of Trent, part 2, chap. 20, no. 8.

58 *LG* 10, 21, 28; *SC* 33; *PO* 2, 12, 13; *AG* 39. The Council uses this expression for the episcopal and presbyteral ministry, because "all that has been said regarding Bishops also applies to priests" (*PO* 4, note 4). The phrase is used eight times, including *gerere personam Christi*—once for bishops and seven times for priests.

59 *Letter* 1980, no. 8. Other letters form a link between the Eucharist and the priest who celebrates it *in persona Christi*: 1979, nos. 3 and 4; 1985, no. 1; 1988, nos. 1, 2, and 6; 1989, no. 8; 1991, no. 3; 1994, no. 1; 1995, no. 3; 1996, no. 4; 2000, no. 5; 2004, no. 2.

60 *Letter* 1985, no. 1, emphasis in the original.

Christi. The Christ whom he makes present and who accomplishes the mystery of the forgiveness of sins is the Christ who appears as the brother of man, the merciful high priest, faithful and compassionate, the shepherd [. . .], the physician [. . .], the one master [. . .], the judge."[61]

In reality, "[t]he ordained ministry, which may never be reduced to its merely functional aspect since it belongs on the level of 'being,' enables the priest to act *in persona Christi*,"[62] "by the power of the Paraclete, of the Holy Spirit."[63] To act *in persona Christi* therefore means to act as "stewards of the mysteries of God" (1 Cor 4:1),[64] "in the celebration of [. . .] our entire sacramental service for the salvation of others."[65]

To act *in persona Christi* also means to act *in nomine Ecclesiae* (in the name of the Church),[66] because Christ is inextricably linked to his Church: "The ministerial priesthood has the task not only of representing Christ [. . .] before the assembly of the faithful, but also of acting in the name of the whole Church when presenting to God the prayer of the Church, and

---

61 Apostolic Exhortation *Reconciliatio et paenitentia* on Reconciliation and Penance in the mission of the Church today (December 2, 1984), no. 29. The *Catechism of the Catholic Church* affirms that priests, in the dispensation of the sacraments, act as "ministers of grace, authorized and empowered by Christ. From Him, they receive the mission and faculty (the sacred power) to act *in persona Christi Capitis* (no. 875)"—in the person of Christ the head. Cf. also *CCC*, nos. 1142, 1548–1551.

62 *Letter* 2004, no. 2. It can be recalled that scholastics say that "being precedes act." Indeed, no one does what he cannot do. By the formula "*in persona Christi*, which assumes necessarily the idea of character as participation in the priesthood of Christ [. . .], the popes also transpose the Christological reference to the level of priestly action, trying to convey the idea that the Christological dimension of the priesthood is what characterizes not only the being but also the doing of the priest." Castellucci, *Il ministero ordinato*, 189. As a result, the priest's identity defines his mission. Thus, "the priest is bound to a special imitation of Christ the Priest, which is the result of the special grace of Orders, the grace of union with Christ the Priest and Victim and, by virtue of this same union, the grace of *good pastoral service to his brothers and sisters*. [. . .] [Priests'] ideal will be to achieve, in Christ, the unity of life" (*General Audience*, May 26, 1993, no. 2, emphasis in the original).

63 *Letter* 1991, no. 3.

64 Cf. *Letter* 1989, no. 8.

65 *Letter* 1991, no. 3. Of course, when the priest acts *in persona Christi* he does so in the well-defined sphere of the spiritual powers conferred by the sacrament of the Holy Orders, that is to say, in the administration of the sacraments and when he preaches and governs by virtue of his ministry.

66 Without a doubt "the relation of the priest to Jesus Christ, and in him to his Church, is found in the very being of the priest by virtue of his sacramental consecration/anointing and in his activity, that is, in his mission or ministry" (*PDV* 16). On this subject, Greshake in his book *Essere preti in questo tempo*, writes an interesting chapter on the historical and theological point of view entitled "The ministry as 'representation' of the Church" (153–85).

above all when offering the Eucharistic sacrifice."[67] Thus, the mission of the priestly ministry is inseparably Christological and ecclesial.

Pastor bonus—The Good Shepherd

The expression *in persona Christi Capitis*—in the person of Christ the head—is linked to the pastoral function of priests. In reality, as John Paul II asserts, it refers to the figure of the Good Shepherd.

> The figure of Jesus Christ as shepherd of the Church, His flock, takes up and represents in new and more evocative terms the same content as that of Jesus Christ as head and servant [. . .]. By virtue of their consecration, priests are configured to Jesus the good shepherd and are called to imitate and to live out his own pastoral charity.[68]

Christ is Head, that is to say, Pastor of his Church. Thus, following Him, whoever received the priestly Order

> is ordained to act in the name of Christ the Head, to bring people into the new life made accessible by Christ, to dispense to them the mysteries—the word, forgiveness, the Bread of Life—to gather them in His body, to help them to form themselves from within, to live and to act according to the saving plan of God. In a word, our identity as priests is manifested in the "creative" exercise of the love for souls communicated by Christ Jesus.[69]

Therefore, to act *in persona Christi* reflects above all the attitude of the Good Shepherd (cf. Jn 10:1–16), because "we are called to show forth the face of the Good Shepherd, and therefore to have the heart of Christ himself."[70] "Here the Good Shepherd, through the presence and voice of the

---

67 *CCC*, no. 1552. "It is because the ministerial priesthood represents Christ that it can represent the Church" (*CCC*, no. 1553).

68 *PDV* 22.

69 *Letter* 1986, no. 10; cf. also *Letter* 1997, no. 5, and *Letter* 2002, no. 1. "According to Jesus' teaching, presiding over the community means serving it, not domineering over it. He himself gave us the example of a shepherd who cares for and serves his flock" (*General Audience*, September 22, 1993, no. 2).

70 *Letter* 2001, no. 11. "In the celebration of this sacrament [of Reconciliation], even more than in the others, it is important that the faithful have an intense experience of the face of Christ the Good Shepherd" (*Letter* 2002, no. 4). Also, "those who, in virtue of priestly ordination, receive from Christ the mission of *shepherds* are called to present anew in their lives and witness to with their actions the heroic love of the *Good Shepherd*" (*General Audience*, July 7, 1993, no. 2, emphasis in the original).

priest, approaches each man and woman."[71] The whole priestly mission must therefore be imbued with this face of Christ.

> Jesus Christ [. . .] has *"made"* shepherds of us too. And it is he who goes about all the cities and villages, *wherever we are sent* in order to perform our priestly and pastoral service. [. . .] It is precisely he, Jesus Christ, who continually feels compassion for the crowds and for every tired and exhausted person, like a "sheep without shepherd" (Cf. Mt 9:36) [. . .] That each of us may learn to serve better, more clearly and more effectively, *his presence as Shepherd* in the midst of the people of today's world![72]

This "configuration" to the Good Shepherd is "in virtue of sacramental Orders and the mandate that the Church confers on them."[73] Truly, priests are "pastors" thanks to the sacrament of Holy Orders, but also through the sacramental link that unites them to the episcopal order.[74] Strictly speaking, the "pastor" is the bishop,[75] because he is the "the one head and pastor of the community, while [the word 'priest'] designates a minister who works in dependence on a bishop."[76]

---

71 *Letter* 2002, no. 9. "The image of the pastor is a synthetic prospective of the ministerial priest-hood, [. . .] the fundamental and unifying element of the ministry and life of the priest, [who] translates with sufficient fidelity the proper style always lived in the presbyterate." Castellucci, *Il ministero ordinato*, 275 (citing a pastoral document of the Italian bishops on the ordained ministry). The Second Vatican Council had said before: "As they fulfill the role of the Good Shepherd, in the very exercise of their pastoral charity [priests] will discover a bond of priestly perfection which draws their life and activity to unity and coordination" (*PO* 14).

72 *Letter* 1984, no. 5, emphasis in the original.

73 *General Audience*, September 22, 1993, no. 1.

74 "Dear Brothers in the Priesthood of Christ, [. . .] in union with your bishops, you are the pastors of the parishes and of the other communities of the People of God in all parts of the world" (*Letter* 1983, no. 4). Already at the Council of Trent, "the ideal of the Bishop and the priest, to which most of the Tridentine Fathers adhered, [was that] the Bishop is by apostolic mission the pastor of his diocese [. . .], of his faithful, and the priests are his auxiliaries" (Castellucci, *Il ministero ordinato*, 121–28). Also, in this voluminous work, Thierry Blot asserts that the geographical delimitation of the parishes was a decisive element in defining the figure of the priest in charge of a parish as pastor of a territory: *Le curé, Pasteur, des origines à la fin du XXe siècle* (Paris: Pierre Téqui, 2000), 89–107.

75 Cf. chap. 2, note 105. It is a "charisma" of his own: "[O]ur priesthood [. . .] enables us, by serving, to guide pastorally the individual *communities* of the People of God, in communion with bishops, who have inherited from the Apostles the pastoral power and charism in the Church" (*Letter* 1985, no. 1, emphasis in the original). "[T]hanks to the priestly character, you share in the *pastoral charism*, which is a sign of a special relationship of *likeness to Christ, the Good Shepherd*. [. . .] you are bearers of the grace of Christ, the eternal Priest, and bearers of the charism of the Good Shepherd. And this you can never forget; this you can never renounce; this you must put into practice at every moment, in every place and in every way" (*Letter* 1979, nos. 5–6).

76 *General Audience*, March 31, 1993, no. 5.

Presbyters are a "support and instrument" of the episcopal order [. . .]. They continue the Bishop's action and in a certain way represent him as pastor in various areas. By virtue of its same pastoral identity and sacramental origin, the ministry of presbyters is clearly exercised "under the authority of the Bishop." [. . .] It is under this authority that they lend "their efforts to the pastoral work of the whole Diocese" by sanctifying and governing that portion of the Lord's flock entrusted to them. It is true that presbyters represent Christ and act in His name [. . .]. However, they can act only as the Bishop's coworkers, thus extending the ministry of the diocesan pastor in the local communities.[77]

For the pope, the image of the Good Shepherd sums up the mission of the priestly ministry. Its function is both to gather and to guide. The first mission is essentially ecclesial, because "pastoral work consists principally in the *service of unity*, that is, in ensuring the union of all in the Body of Christ which is the Church."[78]

The priest can *carry out this social task which is linked with his vocation as a pastor*, that is to say, he can "gather together" the Christian communities to which he is sent. [. . .] [P]riests, exercising [. . .] the function of Christ, [. . .] *gather together God's family* as a brotherhood all of one mind. [. . .] This "gathering together" is service. Each of us must be aware of gathering the community together *not around ourselves but around Christ, and not for ourselves but for Christ*, so that He can act in this community and at the same time in each person. He acts by the power of His Spirit, the Paraclete.[79]

---

77 *General Audience*, August 25, 1993, no. 3. No. 5 of this catechesis continues: "The presbyters' duties towards their bishops are summarized in these words: 'Priests for their part should keep in mind the fullness of the sacrament of Orders which the bishops enjoy and should reverence in their persons the authority of Christ the Supreme Pastor' (*PO 7*)." The fullness of the Holy Orders, received at the episcopate, makes the minister "image" of the Supreme Pastor. In *Letter* 2000, no. 1, the pope addresses "My dear brother priests," and calls their bishops "your Pastors."

78 *General Audience*, May 19, 1993, no. 1, emphasis in the original. "Presbyters serve this vital communion [of the ecclesial community] as pastors in virtue of sacramental Orders and the mandate that the Church confers on them" (*General Audience*, September 22, 1993, no. 1).

79 *Letter* 1989, no. 6, emphasis in the original. The *General Audience* of Wednesday, May 19, 1993, no. 4, adds: "The community dimension of pastoral care [. . .] cannot overlook *the needs of the individual faithful*. [. . .] The Council stresses the need to help each member of the faithful to discover his specific vocation, as a proper characteristic task of the pastor who wants to respect and promote each one's personality. One could say that by His example Jesus Himself, the Good Shepherd who 'calls His own sheep by name' (cf. Jn 10:3–4), has set the standard of individual pastoral care: knowledge and a relationship of friendship with persons."

Then, by gathering those entrusted to him, the priests must exercise the role of guide, that is to say the "pastorality" of their ministry, and "leading the community entrusted to them to the full development of its spiritual and ecclesial life."[80] The life of the Church is "a pilgrimage of faith. Each one of us [. . .] by reason of our priestly vocation and ordination, has a special part in this pilgrimage. As ministers of the Good Shepherd we are called to go forward guiding others, helping them along their way."[81] The purpose of this "pilgrimage" can be summed up by the words that in his 1979 letter the pope already used: "The solicitude of every good shepherd is that all people 'may have life and have it to the full,' (Jn 10:10) so that none of them may be lost, but should have eternal life. Let us endeavour to make this solicitude penetrate deeply into our souls; let us strive to live it."[82]

TRINITARIAN ORIENTATION AND MARIAN DIMENSION OF THE MINISTERIAL PRIESTHOOD

Speaking of the exercise of the priestly ministry, whose sacred celibacy and pastoral actions express important characteristics, John Paul II gives a clear Trinitarian orientation to all priestly action. And he also makes a special connection between the Virgin Mary and the priesthood. I want to address both aspects in this chapter.

The Trinitarian Orientation of the Priestly Ministry

It has been pointed out several times that the priestly mission is directed towards the salvation of souls by making this grace present and effective in

---

For this purpose, "the presbyter who wants to be conformed to the Good Shepherd and reproduce in himself his charity for his brothers and sisters will have to be committed to some very important tasks today [. . .]: to know his own sheep, especially through contacts, visits, relations of friendship, planned or occasional meetings, etc., [. . .]; to welcome, as Jesus did, the people who come to him, ready and available to listen, wanting to understand, [and be] open and genuinely kind, engaging in deeds and activities to aid the poor and unfortunate; to cultivate and practice those 'virtues [such as] goodness of heart, sincerity, strength and constancy of mind, careful attention for justice, courtesy, etc.' (PO 3) [. . .], as well as patience, readiness to forgive [. . .], kindness, affability, the capacity to be obliging and helpful [. . .]. There is a myriad of human and pastoral virtues which the fragrance of Christ's charity can and must determine in the priest's conduct" (General Audience, July 7, 1993, no. 6).

80 General Audience, May 19, 1993, no. 2.

81 Letter 1987, no. 13. The ordained minister exercises this guiding mission by his threefold function of teaching, sanctifying, and governing. Cf. chapter 2 of this work.

82 Letter 1979, no. 7.

the lives of men. That is why it is legitimate to ask ourselves in what sense John Paul II presents this salvation brought to humanity and, ultimately, what it means to be saved: "When in Gethsemane Jesus says: 'Not my will, but yours, be done,' He reveals the truth about the Father and the Father's salvific love for mankind. The 'will of the Father' is precisely salvific love."[83]

The ministerial priesthood is a service of men and at the same time in service to the Father. Indeed, "we carry out this office, through which Christ himself unceasingly 'serves' the Father in the work of our salvation. Our whole priestly existence is and must be deeply imbued with this service."[84] Through this service that Christ continues to render, we are "redeemed [. . .] by His death and made us sharers in immortal life through His resurrection."[85]

> This is the mystery of the Redemption, defined by love. It is the only-begotten Son who takes this love from the Father and who gives it to the Father by bringing it to the world. It is the only-begotten Son who, through this love, gives Himself for the salvation of the world: for the eternal life of all individuals, His brothers and sisters. And we priests, [. . .] we find ourselves particularly close to this redeeming love which the Son has brought to the world—and which He brings continuously. [. . .] The mystery of this redeeming love is [. . .] lastingly inscribed in our vocation and our ministry.[86]

Therefore, to be at the service of salvation means to be at the service of the true life—eternal life—that Jesus has obtained for us by the reconciliation of men with God. But this salvation also means a path forever open to fellowship with God:[87] "God has redeemed us in Jesus Christ for in Him he has granted us the gift of forgiveness. [. . .] God has reconciled the world to Him-

---

83 *Letter* 1987, no. 6. The pope adds in *Letter* 1982, no. 4, "Enable us to love with that love with which Your Father 'loved the world' when He gave 'His only Son, that whoever believes in Him should not perish but have eternal life' (Jn 3:16)."

84 *Letter* 1979, no. 4. To be "as priests 'stewards of the mysteries of God' (1 Cor 4:1) means to place oneself at the disposal of others, and in this way to bear witness to that supreme love which is in Christ, that love which is God himself.

[This] awareness and attitude in the life of each one of us, [. . .] *must constantly broaden and extend to all those whom 'the Father has given us'* (Cf. Jn 17:6). [. . .] Following Jesus' example, the priest, 'the steward of the mysteries of God,' is truly himself when he is 'for others'" (*Letter* 1987, nos. 10–11, emphasis in the original).

85 *Letter* 1980, no. 3.

86 *Letter* 1983, no. 2.

87 A path is offered that gives all "the possibility of becoming adopted sons and daughters of the Eternal Father" (*Letter* 1995, no. 4).

self in Christ. [. . .] The union of man with God has been irreversibly consolidated."[88] In fact, the priest is in charge of accompanying the faithful to the fullness of life in God, of Trinitarian communion, "so that humanity might have access to the depths of God's very life."[89] This is the true life, the "new life": "As the Good Shepherd, [Christ] was about to give his life for his sheep, to save man, to reconcile him with his Father and bring him into a new life."[90]

> The redemption is accomplished through the sacrifice in which Christ—
> the Mediator of the new and eternal covenant—"entered once for all into
> the Holy Place with His own blood," making room in the "house of the
> Father"—in the bosom of the Most Holy Trinity[91]—for all "those who are
> called to the eternal inheritance" (cf. Heb 9:12, 15). It is precisely for this
> reason that the crucified and risen Christ is "the high priest of the good
> things to come" (Heb 9:11) and his sacrifice means a new orientation of
> man's spiritual history.[92]

Christ, Eternal Priest, through his Paschal sacrifice opens for us the possibility of entering into communion with God, the Trinity of Love.[93]

---

88 *Letter* 1983, no. 3.

89 *Letter* 2000, no. 4. The priest gathers so as to direct: "The Council says, 'Exercising the office of Christ, the Shepherd and Head, and according to their share of his authority, priests, in the name of the bishop, gather the family of God together as a brotherhood enlivened by one spirit. Through Christ they lead them in the Holy Spirit to God the Father' (*PO* 6). This is the essential purpose of their activity as pastors and of the authority conferred on them so they may exercise it at their level of responsibility" (*General Audience*, May 19, 1993, no. 2).

90 *Letter* 1986, no. 1. By Baptism, the "anointing with the Holy Spirit first brings about *the supernatural gift* of sanctifying grace by which we become, in Christ, sharers in the divine nature and in the life of the Most Holy Trinity. In each of us, this gift is the interior source of our Christian vocation and of every vocation within the community of the Church, as the People of God of the New Covenant" (*Letter* 1991, no. 1, emphasis in the original).

91 According to the Holy Father "the name 'Abba' [. . .] on Jesus' lips always has a Trinitarian depth" (*Letter* 1987, no. 4).

92 *Letter* 1988, no. 7. "*The Holy Spirit directs the earthly life of Jesus towards the Father*" (*Letter* 1998, no. 1, emphasis in the original) and "the Son wishes to lead us [to the Father] in the Holy Spirit, the Consoler. [. . .] In our ministry, especially our liturgical ministry, we must always be aware that we are on pilgrimage to the Father, guided by the Son in the Holy Spirit. It is precisely to this awareness that we are called by the words with which we conclude every prayer: 'Through our Lord Jesus Christ, your Son, who lives and reigns with you and the Holy Spirit, one God, for ever and ever. Amen'" (*Letter* 1997, no. 2). "The Spirit leads us into the life of the Trinity" (*Letter* 1998, no. 6, heading).

93 In fact, "[t]he great speeches which in John's Gospel follow the washing of the feet and are in some way commentaries upon it, serve as an introduction to the mystery of Trinitarian communion to which we are called by the Father who makes us sharers in Christ by the gift of the Spirit. [. . .] [P]riestly prayer [. . .] shows us Christ in his oneness with the Father, ready to return

Therefore, "to be saved" means not only to receive the true life, being forgiven and reconciled, but this salvation and this new life also mean entering the Trinity already on this earth. In this way,

> the mission of the Son of God reaches its fulfillment when, offering himself, he brings about our adoption as sons and daughters and, by giving the Holy Spirit, makes it possible for human beings to share in the very communion of the Trinity. In the Paschal Mystery, through the Son and in the Holy Spirit, God the Father stoops down to every man and woman, offering the possibility of redemption from sin and liberation from death.[94]

This communion, already real here below, is a foreshadowing of the communion that everyone will live in fullness in the time to come.

> If time is always a movement away from the beginning, it is also, when we think of it, a return to the beginning. And this is of fundamental importance: if time did no more than take us ever further from the beginning, and if its final orientation—the recovery of the origin—were not clear, then our whole existence in time would lack a definite direction. It would have no meaning.
> Christ [. . .] has given direction and meaning to our human passage through time. [. . .] Faith assures us that this journey of Christ to the Father, his Passover, is not an event which involves him alone. We too are called to be part of it. His Passover is our Passover.
> So then, together with Christ we journey towards the Father.[95]

---

to him through the sacrifice of himself, and wanting only that the disciples come to share his unity with the Father: 'As you, Father, are in me and I in you, may they too be one in us' (Jn 17:21)" (*Letter* 2000, no. 4).

94 *Letter* 1999, introduction. One can read in no. 1: "In the Eucharistic celebration we conclude the Opening Prayer with the words: 'Through our Lord Jesus Christ, your Son, who lives and reigns with you, and the Holy Spirit, one God, for ever and ever.' He lives and reigns with you, Father! This conclusion, we may say, has the nature of an ascent: through Christ, in the Holy Spirit, towards the Father."

95 *Letter* 1999, no. 2. The "priest [. . .] together with the faithful entrusted to his pastoral care, walks the path which leads to Christ! [He] yearns to come with them to a true knowledge of the Father and the Son, and so to pass from the experience of the Paraclete's action in history *per speculum in aenigmate* (1 Cor 13:12) to the contemplation of the living and pulsating reality of the Trinity *facie ad faciem* (1 Cor 13:12). He is well aware that he faces 'a long crossing on little boats' and that he soars heavenwards 'on little wings' (Saint Gregory of Nazianzus, *Theological Poems*, 1). But he can also count on the One who set himself to teach the disciples everything" (*Letter* 1998, no. 6). Also, the "Son's vocation to the priesthood expresses the depth of the Trinitarian mystery. For only the Son, the Word of the Father, in whom and through whom all things were created, can unceasingly offer creation in sacrifice to the Father, confirming that every-

The Marian Dimension of the Priestly Ministry

The pope affirms that there is a characteristic link between the Virgin Mary and the ministerial priesthood: "In our 'ministerial' priesthood there is *the wonderful and penetrating dimension of nearness to the Mother of Christ. So let us try to live in that dimension.*"[96] In this, he follows the conciliar constitution on the Church *Lumen Gentium*, in chapter VIII.[97] One can perceive in John Paul II a deepening of this relationship and a theological maturation on this subject: "The profound reason for the presbyter's devotion to Mary most holy is based on the essential relationship established in the divine plan between the Mother of Jesus and the priesthood of her Son's ministers."[98]

Indeed, this maturation[99] is manifested by the fundamental understanding of the typical relationship between Mary and the priesthood.[100] It

---

thing created has come forth from the Father and must become an offering of praise to the Creator" (*Letter* 1996, no. 1).

96 *Letter* 1979, no. 11, emphasis in the original.

97 It seems essential to link this chapter to Mary, who "gave Life to the world" (*LG* 53) and "devoted herself totally as a handmaid of the Lord to the person and work of her Son, under Him and with Him, by the grace of almighty God, serving the mystery of redemption" (*LG* 56). The Holy Virgin "cooperated by her obedience, faith, hope, and burning charity in the work of the Saviour in giving back supernatural life to souls" (*LG* 61) and "continued to bring us the gifts of eternal salvation" (*LG* 62). In contemplating her, the Church understands her maternal mission and "by receiving the Word of God in faith, [she] becomes herself a mother. By her preaching she brings forth to a new and immortal life the sons who are born to her in baptism, conceived of the Holy Spirit and born of God" (*LG* 64). Also, since the priestly ministry has a Marian dimension, it is necessarily linked to the mission of the Church in the world: "The Virgin in her own life lived an example of that maternal love, by which it behooves that all should be animated who cooperate in the apostolic mission of the Church for the regeneration of men" (*LG* 65).

98 *General Audience*, June 30, 1993, no. 1. Pius XI already affirmed, "The priest even more than the faithful should have devotion to Our Lady, for the relation of the priest to Christ is more deeply and truly like that which Mary bears to her Divine Son." Encyclical *Ad Catholici Sacerdotii* (December 20, 1935), no. 39.

99 Cf. Sacred Congregation for Catholic Education, *Circular Letter Concerning Some of the More Urgent Aspects of Spiritual Formation in Seminaries* (January 6, 1980). One can read, at no. 4: "The Church has slowly become aware of the Marian mystery. Far from having herself added to what Scripture taught us, she met the Virgin Mary in each of the stages in which she sought to discover Christ. Christology is also a Mariology."

100 René Laurentin examined this report in his work *Maria—ecclesia—sacerdotium*. The parallels between Mary and the priesthood are not new. The analogy prevails at the mission level. In this sense, Paul VI said, during a General Audience, October 7, 1964: "What relationships and what distinctions exist between the motherhood of Mary [. . .] and the apostolic priesthood, constituted by the Lord to be the instrument of salvific communication between God and men? Mary gives Christ to humanity; and the priesthood also gives Christ to humanity, but in a different way, of course; Mary, by the Incarnation and by the bestowal of grace, of which God has filled

is not a "simple devotion," however laudable, but an intrinsically necessary and objective link.

> Mary's relationship to the priesthood derives primarily from the fact of her motherhood. Becoming the Mother of Christ by her consent to the angel's message, Mary became the Mother of the High Priest. [...] [T]he Virgin Mary expressed the same attitude, saying 'Behold, I am the handmaid of the Lord. May it be done to me according to your word.' This perfect correspondence shows us that a close relationship has been established between Mary's motherhood and Christ's priesthood. By that very fact a special bond exists between the priestly ministry and Mary most holy.[101]

Moreover, Jesus specifically entrusted his mother to a "priest," the Apostle John, who had received in the Cenacle—with the other Apostles—the mission to perpetuate under sacramental form the redemptive Sacrifice.

> The Apostle John [...] was one of the "Twelve" to whom the Master addressed, together with the words instituting the Eucharist, the command: "Do this in memory of me." He received the power to celebrate the Eucharistic sacrifice instituted in the Upper Room on the eve of the passion [...]. At the moment of death, Jesus gives his own Mother to this disciple. John "took her to his own home." [...] And so, by taking "to his own home" the Mother who stood beneath her Son's cross, he also made his own all that was within her on Golgotha [...]. All this—the superhuman experience of the sacrifice of our redemption, inscribed in the heart of Christ the Redeemer's own Mother—was entrusted to the man who in the Upper Room received the power to make this sacrifice present through the priestly ministry of the Eucharist.
>
> Does this not have special eloquence for each of us? If John at the foot of the cross somehow represents every man and woman [...] how much more does this concern each of us, who are sacramentally called to the priestly ministry of the Eucharist in the Church![102]

---

it; the priesthood, by the powers of the Sacred Order. The first has a ministry that gives birth to Christ in the flesh [...]; the second is a sacramental and external ministry, which dispenses these gifts of truth and grace and this Spirit, who carries and forms the mystical Christ in souls who accept the service of salvation from the priestly hierarchy. But of course Mary is, after Christ and by virtue of Christ, at the summit of this economy of salvation: she precedes and surpasses the priesthood" (translation mine).

101 *General Audience*, June 30, 1993, no. 2.

102 *Letter* 1988, no. 3.

In fact, this "closeness," to which John Paul II alludes in his 1979 letter, is related to the maternal being and function of Mary for the being and mission of the priesthood of her Son. It is because she is the mother of the Sovereign Priest that she is also particularly close to those who act in the name of her Son. Christ associated and continues to associate His Mother with the work of redemption.[103] It relates to a sacerdotal proximity, or better, a sacerdotal maternity of Mary.

From these remarks one can conclude that Mary is no stranger to the ministerial priesthood, nor reduced to a "decorative" element, linked to pious sentiments or custom. She is an essential element. Certainly, there is not an ontological relationship between the ordained minister and the Mother of the Savior, as it is between the priest and the priesthood of Christ.[104] The priest is a "sacrament" of Christ, his living "memory." And if so, the relationship between Mary and her Son must also find a "sacramental" expression in the priestly ministry.[105]

---

103 Cf. *LG* 55–62.

104 John Paul II said: "The presbyter [. . .] looks to [Mary] as the perfect model of his life and ministry, because she is the one, as the Council says, who 'under the guidance of the Holy Spirit made a total dedication of herself for the mystery of human redemption' (*PO 18*)" (*General Audience*, June 30, 1993, no. 6). In my opinion, Mary, having not received the ministerial priesthood, could not be proposed as a "model of ministry" for the priest, because his only model is the Christ Priest and Pastor. The devotion to *Virgo sacerdos*, developed by Ferdinand Chirino de Salazar (+ 1646) and taken over by the *École Française*, came to an end in 1913 when the cardinals of the Holy Office rejected this devotion and its iconographic representation. However, there is a double relationship between the priest and the Holy Virgin. First of all, she is Mother and perfect prototype of the Church. In this perspective, the ordained minister sees in her—and exemplarily—her model of communion with God, of the spiritual offering of her life and of praise, as well as the proclamation and service of the Word. Then, the second relationship—which will be developed later—is established objectively between Mary and the ministerial priesthood, thanks to the words of Christ on the Cross: "Behold your Mother." "According to some scholars, the first to interpret the words of the Lord 'Behold, your Mother [. . .]; behold, your son,' in the sense of Mary's spiritual motherhood towards the disciples of the Lord was Origen, in the introduction to his monumental commentary on the Gospel of Saint John." Graziano Borgonovo, *Giovanni Paolo II e la formazione sacerdotale* (Siena: Cantagalli, 2007), 146.

105 Since the priest is "another Christ," the exercise of Mary's motherhood with regard to those who are configured to her Son is different from the spiritual motherhood of the other faithful. It is an effective cooperative relationship and, according to *LG* 62, a "salvific duty. [. . .] [B]y her constant intercession [she] continued to bring us the gifts of eternal salvation. By her maternal charity, she cares for the brethren of her Son, who still journey on earth surrounded by dangers and cultics, until they are led into the happiness of their true home. [. . .] The unique mediation of the Redeemer does not exclude but rather gives rise to a manifold cooperation which is but a sharing in this one source." And also, at no. 63 of this constitution: "The Son whom she brought forth is He whom God placed as the first-born among many brethren, namely the faithful, in whose birth and education she cooperates with a maternal love." The only conciliar document that makes an explicit link between the Virgin Mary and the priestly ministry is *Presbyterorum*

Certainly, the Blessed Virgin, having participated in the mystery of Christ and the fulfillment of his priesthood, must also participate in the priestly ministry. This is the logical conclusion to which the Holy Father leads us. There is, therefore, a closeness to Mary who actively participates in the priestly ministry. This relationship is not only analogous or devotional but existential because of her maternity to the One who is the High Priest. John Paul II allows us to understand more deeply that Mary is at the service of Christ.[106] Through her presence with the minister, she reminds the minister of the faith and love with which Christ must be made present in the Church and by the Church.

This close relationship has concrete implications for three aspects of priestly life and ministry: kerygmatic and cultural (proclamation of the Word and celebration of worship), pastoral (guide to salvation), and maternal (instrument of grace and divine filiation).

Kerygmatic and Cultic Ministry

Mary is close to the priestly ministry and foremost in its kerygmatic aspect. Definitively, this ministry is a service of announcement and transmission of the mystery of Christ. Thus, "the priest should very often turn to Mary, the Mother of God, who received the Word of God with perfect faith."[107]

In fact, by receiving the Word, the Word of God, through her response to the call of God, the Blessed Virgin "became both the servant and the disciple of the Word to the point of conceiving, in her heart and in her

---

Ordinis, no. 18: from the docility to the mission that the priests assumed in the Holy Spirit, they "will always find a wonderful example of such docility in the Blessed Virgin Mary, who was led by the Holy Spirit to dedicate herself totally to the mystery of man's redemption. Let priests love and venerate with filial devotion and veneration this mother of the Eternal High Priest, Queen of Apostles and Protector of their own ministry."

106 Of course, "as we know, the Blessed Virgin fulfilled her role of mother not only in physically begetting Jesus but also in his moral formation. In virtue of her motherhood, she was responsible for raising the child Jesus in a way appropriate to his priestly mission, the meaning of which she learned from the message of the Incarnation.

In Mary's consent we can recognize an assent to the substantial truth of Christ's priesthood and the willingness to cooperate in fulfilling it in the world. This lays the objective basis for the role Mary was called to play, too, in the formation of Christ's ministers, sharers in his priesthood" (*General Audience*, June 30, 1993, no. 3).

107 *General Audience*, June 30, 1993, no. 1. "The Virgin [. . .] will lead him down the ways of evangelical obedience, that the Paraclete may draw him, beyond all his own plans, towards total acceptance of the mind of God" and his Word of Truth (*Letter* 1998, no. 7).

flesh, the Word made man, so as to give him to mankind."[108] So, for this reason,

> in the midst of the People of God, that looks to Mary with immense love and hope, you must look to her with exceptional hope and love. Indeed, you must proclaim Christ who is her Son; and who will better communicate to you the truth about him than his Mother? You must nourish human hearts with Christ: and who can make you more aware of what you are doing than she who nourished him?[109]

On the other hand, this closeness to Mary—which for the priest necessarily means "taking Mary into his home [. . .] finding a place for her in his own life, remaining in habitual union with her in thoughts, feelings, zeal for the kingdom of God and for devotion to her"[110]—has implications for the celebration of worship,[111] especially the Holy Eucharist. Mary is "woman of the Eucharist,"[112] and therefore, "who more than Mary can help us taste the greatness of the Eucharistic mystery? She more than anyone can teach us how to celebrate the sacred mysteries with due fervour and to commune with her Son, hidden in the Eucharist."[113]

Pastoral Ministry

The presence of the Holy Virgin with the ordained minister also refers to his pastoral mission: "Mary was uniquely associated with Christ's priestly sacrifice, sharing His will to save the world by the Cross. [. . .] She can obtain and give to those who share in her Son's priesthood on the ministerial level the grace moving them to respond ever more fully to the demands of spir-

---

108 *PDV* 82.

109 *Letter* 1979, no. 11.

110 *General Audience*, June 30, 1993, no. 5.

111 Faith is born from the proclamation of the Word of God and leads to the celebration of the holy mysteries. Cf. Rom 10:14–17.

112 *Ecclesia de Eucharistia*, no. 53.

113 *Letter* 2005, no. 8. Of course, one can expand these words to other sacramental celebrations, which are signs of salvation. Mary is with the priest when he administers Baptism and Confirmation, because she is the Mother of Divine Grace and Spouse of the Holy Spirit; she is also close to the ordained minister when he dispenses the "sacraments of healing" (Reconciliation and Anointing of the Sick), because she is Mother of Mercy and Health of the Sick; but also when he blesses the love of the spouses in the sacrament of Marriage, for she is Mother Most Chaste. For these Marian titles, cf. *Litaniae Lauretanae*.

itual oblation that the priesthood entails."[114] Indeed, the mission of the priest is a service that aims to lead to eternal salvation.[115]

> Beside *Christ the Servant,* we cannot forget the one who is "the Handmaid," Mary. St. Luke tells us that, at the decisive moment of the Annunciation, the Virgin expressed her *fiat* in these words: "Behold, I am the handmaid of the Lord" (Lk 1:38). [. . .] If the priesthood is by its nature ministerial, we must live it in union *with the Mother who is the Handmaid of the Lord.* Then our priesthood will be kept safe in her hands, indeed in her heart, and we shall be able to open it to everyone. In this way our priesthood, in all its dimensions, will be fruitful and salvific.[116]

This function of guide, proper to the priestly ministry, requires from the pastor of souls[117] a certain spiritual sensitivity and particular attention to the "signs of the times."[118] Thus,

> The Virgin [. . .] will prepare him to listen humbly and sincerely to his brothers and sisters, that he may recognize in the drama of their lives and their aspirations the "groans of the Spirit" (cf. Rom 8:26). She will enable the priest to serve them with enlightened discretion, that he may teach them the values of the Gospel. She will make him diligent in searching for "the things that are above" (Col 3:1), that he may witness convincingly to the primacy of God.[119]

---

114 *General Audience,* June 30, 1993, no. 4.

115 Cf. *Homily* 1984, no. 2: "Today's liturgy reminds us that we are in a special way 'servants of Christ and stewards of the mysteries of God' (1 Cor 4:1), that we are *men of the divine economy of salvation.*" Emphasis in the original. Mary preceded us "in her pilgrimage of faith through her perfect union with her Son unto the cross and goes before, presenting herself in an eminent and singular way to the whole People of God, which follows the same path, in the footsteps of Christ in the Holy Spirit. Should not we priests unite ourselves with her in a special way, we who as pastors of the Church must also lead the communities entrusted to us along the path which from the Upper Room of Pentecost follows Christ throughout human history?" (*Letter* 1988, no. 7). The path she has traveled and her place with God become for the Church a beacon that leads it safely into harbor, helping priests in the fulfillment of their specific mission for the people of God. Cf. *LG* 62 and 68.

116 *Letter* 1995, no. 8, emphasis in the original.

117 In the conciliar sense, to exercise the office of pastor or government means above all to lead souls to God (cf. *PO* 6), a function that every priest must perform. Indeed, even those who do not have an ecclesiastical office receive this mission so that "the faithful are led individually in the Holy Spirit to a development of their own vocation according to the Gospel" (*PO* 6).

118 *GS* 4.

119 *Letter* 1998, no. 7.

It is for this reason that the priest "to her confides and entrusts himself and his pastoral ministry, asking her to make it yield abundant fruit."[120]

Mother's Ministry: Fertile Virginity

In his mission, the priest is charged with bringing men to the divine life of grace and nourishing it, as a mother brings her child into the world. If this affirmation finds a particular logic in the relationship that can be established between priesthood and motherhood, John Paul II introduces a new reflection: the relationship of celibacy to maternity. For just as Mary is both a virgin and a mother, the priest also expresses a similar reality by his celibacy, the call to be fruitful.[121] Indeed, "[t]he Virgin will help the priest to welcome the gift of chastity as the expression of a greater love which the Spirit awakens so that the love of God may come to birth in a host of brothers and sisters."[122]

> [T]here must be developed in our life this fatherhood "according to the Spirit," which is one of the results of "making ourselves eunuchs for the sake of the kingdom of God."[123]

Thus, the mission of the priest is easily found to be in consonance with the burden of a mother, because his ministry becomes by the fulfillment of his office an instrument of grace and divine filiation. Surely,

> this "spiritual fatherhood" [. . .] on the human level is similar to motherhood. Moreover, does not God himself, the Creator and Father, make the comparison between his love and the love of a human mother (cf. Is 49:15;

---

120 *General Audience*, June 30, 1993, no. 6.

121 "In Mary, who is the Immaculate Virgin, we also discover *the mystery* of that supernatural *fruitfulness through the power of the Holy Spirit*" (*Letter* 1987, no. 13, emphasis in the original).

122 *Letter* 1998, no. 7. The analogy with Mary, Virgin and Mother, is above all established with the Church (cf. *LG* 64; cf. also *PO* 6, on the maternal role of the ecclesial community): "Mary is the Virgin Mother, and when the Church turns to Mary, figure of the Church, she recognizes herself in Mary because the Church too is 'called mother and virgin.' The Church is virgin, because she guards whole and pure the faith given to the Spouse" (*Letter* 1988, no. 5). However, continues the pope, this analogy concerns us in a particular way: "The analogy between the Church and the Virgin Mother has a special eloquence for us, who link our priestly vocation to celibacy, that is, to 'making ourselves eunuchs for the sake of the kingdom of heaven.' We recall the conversation with the apostles, in which Christ explained to them the meaning of this choice (cf. Mt 19:12) and we seek to understand the reasons fully. [. . .] By reason of this model—yes, of the prototype which the Church finds in Mary—it is necessary that our priestly choice of celibacy for the whole of our lives should also be placed within her heart. We must have recourse to this Virgin Mother when we meet difficulties along our chosen path" (*Letter* 1988, no. 5).

123 *Letter* 1988, no. 5.

66:13)? Thus we are speaking of a characteristic of our priestly personality that expresses precisely apostolic maturity and spiritual "fruitfulness." If the whole Church "learns her own motherhood from Mary" (Cf. Encyclical *Redemptoris Mater*, no. 43), do we not need to do so as well?[124]

Pastoral ministry can encounter many difficulties and obstacles, but it is also a cause for great joy.[125]

> It is worth recalling these scriptural references,[126] so that the truth about the Church's motherhood, founded on the example of the Mother of God, may become more and more a part of our priestly consciousness. [We] live the equivalent of this *spiritual motherhood* in a manly way, namely, as a *"spiritual fatherhood"* [. . .]. Is not Paul's analogy on "pain in childbirth" close to all of us in the many situations in which we too are involved in the spiritual process of man's *"generation"* and *"regeneration"* by the power of the Holy Spirit, the Giver of life?[127]

Finally, this "priestly motherhood" is expressed by the care that the ordained minister must have with regard to "his children." He must above all nourish them[128] through the Word and the sacraments, especially the Eucharist: "When, in the Letter to the Ephesians, we read about Christ as the Spouse who 'nourishes and cherishes' the Church as His body (cf. 5:29), we cannot fail to link this spousal solicitude on the part of Christ above all with the gift of Eucharistic food, similar to the many maternal concerns associated with 'nourishing and cherishing' a child."[129]

SYNTHESIS

In studying the function of the ordained minister, it can be resolutely concluded with a determination that stems from all that has been affirmed, that the priest is the "memory" of Christ, because the ministerial priesthood is the "sacrament" of the mediation of Christ. Indeed, since ontologically the sacramental ordina-

---

124 *Letter* 1988, no. 4.

125 *Letter* 1987, no. 13.

126 For the sake of clarity, I transcribed texts quoted by the Holy Father in this *Letter* 1988, no. 4: "the children with whom I am again in travail" (Gal 4:19) and a mother "nourishing and cherishing" a child (cf. Gal 5:29).

127 *Letter* 1988, no. 4.

128 As the Holy Father says: "You must nourish human hearts with Christ" (*Letter* 1979, no. 11).

129 *Letter* 1988, no. 4.

tion transforms the one who receives it, it follows that his priestly action makes present, as a visible sign, the presence of the Savior: "I live, no longer I, but Christ lives in me" (Gal 2:20). Being and acting are inseparable; one cannot act in the name of Christ and produce the effects of salvation, unless as one empowered by this particular consecration. The ministerial priesthood has the mission given by the Savior Himself to manifest, in the most distinct times and places, the presence and action of Christ in favor of men.

This is why sacred celibacy is a visible sign of the virginal and nuptial love with which Christ loves his Father and the Church. Here again, it is significant to see the coherence in the thought of John Paul II: the priestly vocation is always built with relation to God, as well as in relation to men. Therefore, the charism of celibacy is profoundly suited to the ordained ministry, as adoption of the *forma vivendi Christi*, Christ's form of life. In Him is rooted the truth of love as a total gift of self and a necessary relationship to others. The priest's first and principal mission is to make present with his life this exclusive love of God and men.

Celibacy thus becomes an expression of pastoral charity and consequently—according to the vision of the Holy Father—the priest is "memory" of the pastoral care of the Lord in regard to souls. The ordained minister receives the mission to act *in persona Christi, Pastor bonus*—in the person of Christ, the Good Shepherd. Configured to Christ, he can say with Him: "I am the Good Shepherd. A good shepherd lays down his life for the sheep" (Jn 10:11). In this way, the Church recognizes Christ sacramentally present in an effective sign—the priest—who refers to Him only and to His authority. And through this sign, she concretely experiences in her life that Christ Himself is her Lord and that He continues to guide and attend to her, through the functions that He guarantees to be effective.

The mission of the priest also has a maternal connotation, because it must engender divine life: "I am again in labor until Christ be formed in you" (Gal 4:19). But the prodigality of a mother is not limited to giving life; it also maintains and nourishes that life. Likewise, the ordained minister nourishes the life of grace by lovingly proclaiming the Word that gives life and by administering the sacraments. The final orientation, the eschatological orientation, is the Trinitarian communion as prototype. The Church is already on this earth as its icon.[130]

---

130 It can be remembered that "[f]or the purpose of assisting the work of the common priesthood of the faithful, other particular ministries also exist, not consecrated by the sacrament of Holy

In view of all this, one can sustain, interpreting the pope's thought, that the mission of the ministerial priesthood is subordinate to the common priesthood and exists according to it. This is not an affirmation that one spontaneously integrates. However, it seems that the magisterium of John Paul II is clear on this subject. The priestly ministry is ordered to the service of the baptismal priesthood: a means par excellence and indispensable, by which Christ makes Himself present in the Church.[131] By this means, the priestly existence of Christians reaches more easily its fullness, its perfection of charity, that is to say, its holiness and eternal happiness.[132] Therefore, the more the baptized become aware of their own dignity and their call, the more they will feel the need for priests. Ultimately, the sacrament of Holy Orders is an inestimable gift that God gives to the Church.

Orders; their functions are determined by the bishops, in accord with liturgical traditions and pastoral needs" (*CCC*, no. 1143).

Cf. Bruno Forte, *The Church: Icon of the Trinity. A Brief Study* (Boston: Pauline Books, 1991). Cf. also Congregation for the Doctrine of Faith, *Letter to Bishops of the Catholic Church on Some Aspects of the Church understood as Communion—Communionis Notio* (May 28, 1992).

131 Cardinal Christoph Schönborn said on September 28, 2009, at the International Retreat for Priests (September 27–October 3, 2009, Ars, France): "The ministerial priesthood is of the order of *ea quae sunt ad finem*, as Saint Thomas Aquinas would say: it is about the means. The means are not the end. They serve the end. The end of the works of God is our eternal happiness, our beatitude. All that unfolds the potentialities of baptismal grace, all that brings about our union with Christ, brings us closer to the blessed end of our full participation in the divine life. The ministerial priesthood is one of the means to realize the end for which God created us and for which Christ redeemed us."

132 Cf. *CCC*, no. 1.

Conclusion

L et us highlight the main elements of this research. This conclusion is an attempt to answer with conviction the initial question that guided us throughout this work, but also from the perspective of openness: What teaching did John Paul II give us regarding the ministerial priesthood in the historical context throughout the Church?

First, in the discourse on the ministerial priesthood, it seems essential to me to affirm that John Paul II recalls the necessity of maintaining the primacy of the Christological reference (chapter 1), because any consideration of the priesthood must start from Christ the Priest.[1] This reference makes us understand that the new priesthood is not the purview of human appropriation or the order of a ministry delegated by a group of people, but a gift of God who elects those whom He wills. Also, the priesthood is that of Christ Himself, and the priest acts *in persona Christi* and, therefore, as a sacrament of His mediation, especially in the celebration of the sacraments. He is in the Church and is before her as a sign and a personal and visible instrument of the primacy of Christ and His authority, which builds the community.[2] The ordained minister participates "in the 'consecration/ anointing' and in the 'mission' of Christ. [He continues] Christ's prayer, word, sacrifice and salvific action in the Church."[3]

In the second place, the fundamental reference of the priestly ministry to the Eucharist must be maintained, without falling into a purely cultic perspective, because the priesthood was born with the Eucharist, as entrusted by Jesus Christ to the twelve Apostles (chapter 2). This means that the Eucharist is the summit in the life of the Christian community but also of the ordained minister who fulfills the service of the pastoral presidency. This relationship is essentially ecclesiological, because *Ecclesia de Eucharistia vivet*,[4] and by communion with this mystery the Church is built as the

---

1 "The priest finds the full truth of his identity in being a derivation, a specific participation in and continuation of Christ himself, the one high priest of the new and eternal covenant" (*PDV* 12).

2 This authority is a service, and in its original sense, its purpose is to help someone grow (cf. *PO* 2 and 9).

3 *PDV* 16, citing Synod of Bishops, Eighth Ordinary General Assembly, "The Formation of Priests in the Circumstances of the Present Day," (1990) Instrumentum Laboris, 16; cf. Proposition 7.

4 Title of the fourteenth encyclical of John Paul II, dated April 17, 2003.

body of Christ. From the Eucharist springs the strength necessary for the Church to fulfill her mission of salvation, and toward it converges all action.

As a third point, I underscore that the teaching of John Paul II emphasizes the ministerial and pastoral dimension of the priesthood (chapter 3). Fortunately, the time has passed when the sacrament of Holy Orders was perceived as a personal dignity or a means of individual sanctification. The ministerial priesthood is much more than that, because it is an ecclesial diakonia, a ministry in the Church and for it, in order to energize and lead the common priesthood of all the faithful to its fullness. Thus, one could say that the ordained minister must be invested with the charism of service in the form of pastoral charity, in a missionary and ecclesial apostolic perspective, a vision that inspires his ministry and his entire life.

These three conclusions refer to the notions of vocation (chapter 1), consecration (chapter 2), and mission (chapter 3) which, finally, are three integral elements of the same reality, the priestly being. These elements are considered the axis of the priestly ministry. To be configured to Christ implies a necessary cooperation of man, particularly through the exercise of ministry. In his own life, the priest must increasingly make visible the life of Christ; hence the question: How can the understanding of this requirement shape a priestly spirituality, which determines his human conduct, in its moral and pastoral aspects? Priesthood implies an integrity of life and service. How can this be reflected without separating what it *is* from what it *does*? An authentic priestly spirituality can only lead to the unity of life evoked in *Presbyterorum Ordinis*, no. 14. This would prevent the priest from all forms of clericalism, denounced by John Paul II as a "harmful" distortion of government, that becomes more about "power than service."[5]

In addition, it would be exciting to further deepen the Trinitarian dimension of the priestly ministry present in the writings of John Paul II. This aspect is discreetly perceptible in this study. In fact, when referring to the priesthood of Christ, John Paul II speaks of the Father who sends the Son and consecrates Him by the anointing of the Holy Spirit (chapter 1). The source of the priesthood is trinitarian. From there, the priest acts *in persona Christi* thanks to the gift of the Holy Spirit granted by the Father during the epiclesis addressed to him by the Church. Also, Jesus announces the coming of the Kingdom by the force of the Spirit (cf. Lk 4: 18) and leads us to communion with his Father: "Father, they are your gift to me. I wish

---

5 John Paul II, *Address to the Bishops of the Antilles on Their Ad limina Visit* (May 7, 2002).

that where I am they also may be with me" (Jn 17:24, cf. also Jn 10:29, 13:3, 14:2). This Trinitarian dimension could open up relationships between John Paul II's thinking and the Eastern theological tradition. Could the pneumatological aspect of the priesthood, highlighted by the Holy Father, be a place of exchange and mutual enrichment with the East in what relates to the field of priestly ministry?

After the third-longest pontificate in the history of the Church, John Paul II has provided to anyone who would like to research more about the ordained ministry an abundant source of documents beyond the scope of this work. I think, for example, of his homilies giving during priestly and episcopal ordinations, of his speeches made during the *ad limina apostolorum* visits, of his speeches during his apostolic journeys and on other journeys. This is why, in addition to the themes just mentioned, one would certainly discover a profusion of relevant subjects open to further research on the Catholic priesthood. By his magisterium, the Polish pope testified to his fidelity to the deposit of faith, while deepening certain subjects by his docility to the Spirit who leads the Church towards a deeper understanding of revealed truth (cf. Jn 16:13).

Afterword to the English Edition

When I published the first edition of this book in Portuguese in 2018, the subject matter and approach were easily accepted. John Paul II, one of the longest reigning popes in history, had been canonized by Pope Francis in 2014 and had laid down a definitive path guiding the Church's Magisterium in the implementation of the Second Vatican Council, including on the subject of the priesthood. However, in 2020, as we were preparing this English edition, the "McCarrick Report" was published, and a heavy salvo of articles called the pontificate of John Paul II into question. This recalled a similar situation, still present in the collective memory, of Marcial Maciel Degollado, the disgraced founder of the Legionaries of Christ. Many were those, some very close to John Paul II, who rose to reaffirm that he always placed himself before the Lord and made decisions not only in conscience but also in the presence of God in the Tabernacle. While this does not mean that his decisions could not have been wrong, it does show that John Paul II never made a decision lightly.

For those who seek holiness through the path of the Church, a doubt still remains about whether these incidents taint the pope's legacy. To this end, it is worth remembering that even if the Church has the divine prerogative of indefectibility, and he who is elected to the Chair of Peter enjoys the charism of infallibility, nonetheless every saint remains a creature limited by his human condition. History has seen others. The task of a pope is not necessarily to work to be canonized, of course, but to confirm believers in the faith. This is what doctrinally orthodox popes have done despite personal weaknesses, while other morally upright popes who were irreproachable and who lived as ascetics nevertheless dispersed errors that, instead of affirming in the faith, disoriented the faithful. Then there is another category of popes who are virtuous and doctrinally orthodox like John Paul II, and with them there is instead a danger of thinking that the canonization of their life and witness also canonizes their every single decision and judgment. Examining the particulars of these cases would be too much in this brief space, but we simply should keep in mind that his overall holiness and virtue were evident and have been confirmed by the Church, and that he himself, like all Christians, knew he was a sinner and continually implored the Lord for mercy.

The purpose of this book is to promote Pope John Paul II's teaching to laypeople who recognize the gift of the ministerial priesthood and for the priests who take their call seriously. The pope always demonstrated great esteem for the priestly ministry and from the beginning of his pontificate showed particular attention to priests, to whom from 1979 onward he sent annually his famous letters on the occasion of Holy Thursday. So we ask: Did John Paul II's vision of the ordained ministry help or encourage the attitude of clericalism that Pope Francis sees as discouraging most priests and bishops from exposing and expelling those predators who used the priesthood to satisfy perverse inclinations? Such a clericalism—which instinctively believes and protects brother priests and distrusts and minimizes concerns from the laity—could be a temptation for every priest, but it is within each priest's power to support or oppose it.

In fact, on the level of personal attitudes and habits, John Paul II's magisterium provides the antidote for the attitude that refuses to sacrifice for or to listen to the laity. He often reminded priests of the need for personal holiness of life consistent with the clerical state, supported by a deep spiritual life and based on proven human maturity. Also, as a great promoter of the role of the laity since the time of the Second Vatican Council, John Paul II placed the ministerial priesthood at the service of all in the Church communion. From his early ministry on, he gave an example of being close to the laity, above all families and youth, learning from their Christian experience.

The first letter to priests, on April 8, 1979, was like a paradigmatic program of interior reformation for the clergy. John Paul II wrote: "Every day we have to be converted anew. [. . .] Being converted means, for us, seeking again the pardon and strength of God in the sacrament of Reconciliation, and thus always beginning anew, and every day progressing, overcoming ourselves, making spiritual conquests, giving cheerfully. [. . .] *[P]rayer is the first and last condition for conversion*."[1] Twenty years later, on the eve of the Jubilee Year, he said, "ordained ministers [. . .] themselves must be converted."[2] Effectively, for the pope, clericalism does not have a place in Holy Orders: "The ministerial priesthood, in Christ's plan, is an expression not of *domination* but of *service*" and must be lived "*with the Mother who is the Handmaid of the Lord*."[3] For this reason, "the human dimension of priestly

1 *Letter* 1979, no. 10, emphasis in the original.

2 *Letter* 1999, no. 6.

3 *Letter* 1995, no. 8.

service, in order to be fully authentic, must be rooted in God."[4] Acknowledging that sins and infidelity of clergy disfigure the immaculate Church, he prayed in solidarity with his brother priests: "We ask You, [oh Lord], to forgive all our faults towards this holy mystery which is your priesthood in our life."[5]

This book, although limited to a few of his writings, shows how much the Polish pope's teaching is based on the traditional faith of the Church on this subject and how he deepens it. Also, the life of John Paul II is a reflection of his teaching, showing how he himself lived it as a priest, bishop, and pope.

Saint John Paul II, protect the Church you have served with such holiness!

---

4 *Letter* 1991, no. 2.

5 *Letter* 1993, reflections. https://www.vatican.va/content/john-paul-ii/fr/letters/1993/documents/hf_jp-ii_let_08041993_priests.html. Accessed July 27, 2021. These reflections are only available with the French version of the text.

Bibliography

1. PONTIFICAL, HOLY SEE, AND LITURGICAL SOURCES
1.1. Magisterium of Saint John Paul II

a. Documents

Encyclical Letter *Redemptor Hominis*. March 4, 1979.

Letter *Dominicæ Cenæ* on the Mystery and Worship of the Eucharist. February 24, 1980.

Apostolic Exhortation *Reconciliatio et paenitentia* on Reconciliation and Penance in the Mission of the Church Today. December 2, 1984.

Encyclical Letter *Dominum et vivificantem* on the Holy Spirit in the Life of the Church and the World. May 18, 1986.

Apostolic Exhortation *Christifideles laici* on the Vocation and Mission of the Lay Faithful in the Church and in the World. December 30, 1988.

Apostolic Exhortation *Pastores dabo vobis* on the Formation of Priests in the Circumstances of the Present Day. March 25, 1992.

Encyclical Letter *Ecclesia de Eucharistia* on the Eucharist in its Relationship to the Church. April 17, 2003.

b. Letters, Homilies, and Audiences

Chrism Mass Homily. April 16, 1981.

Homily for World Jubilee of Clergy. February 23, 1984.

General Audiences: March 31, 1993; April 21, 1993; May 5, 1993; May 12, 1993; May 19, 1993; May 26, 1993; June 2, 1993; June 9, 1993; June 30, 1993; July 7, 1993; July 17, 1993; July 21, 1993; July 28, 1993; August 4, 1993; August 25, 1993; September 1, 1993; September 22, 1993; September 29, 1993; October 6, 1993.

Address to the Bishops of the Antilles on Their Ad Limina Visit. May 7, 2002.

Chrism Mass Homily. April 17, 2003.

Letters to My Brother Priests. Downers Grove, Ill.: Midwest Theological Forum, 2006.

c. Books

Gift and Mystery: On the Fiftieth Anniversary of My Priestly Ordination. New York: Image Books, 1996.

Rise, Let Us Be on Our Way! New York: Warner Books, 2004.

Memory and Identity: Personal Reflections. London: Weidenfeld & Nicolson, 2005.

1.2. Documents of the Holy See

Congregation for the Doctrine of Faith. *Letter to Bishops of the Catholic Church on Certain Questions Concerning the Minister of the Eucharist—Sacerdotium ministeriale.* August 6, 1983.

_____. *Letter to Bishops of the Catholic Church on Some Aspects of the Church understood as Communion—Communionis Notio.* May 28, 1992.

_____. *Letter to Bishops of the Catholic Church on the Collaboration of Men and Women in the Church and in the World.* July 31, 2004.

Congregation for Bishops. *Directory for the Pastoral Ministry of Bishops—Apostolorum Successores.* February 22, 2004.

Congregation for the Clergy. *Directory on the Ministry and Life of Priests.* January 31, 1994.

_____. *Instruction on Certain Questions Regarding the Collaboration of the Non-Ordained Faithful in the Sacred Ministry of Priest.* August 15, 1997.

_____. Instruction. *The Priest, Pastor and Leader of the Parish Community.* August 4, 2002.

_____. *The Eucharist and the Priest.* June 27, 2003.

Congregation for Catholic Education. *A Guide to Formation in Priestly Celibacy.* April 2, 1974.

_____. *Circular Letter Concerning Some of the More Urgent Aspects of Spiritual Formation in Seminaries.* January 6, 1980.

1.3. Liturgical Books

The Roman Pontifical of Ordination. Washington, D.C.: United States Conference of Catholic Bishops, 2003.

The Roman Missal. New Jersey: Catholic Book Publishing, 2011.

2. OTHERS

Acerbi, Antonio. "Osservazioni sulla formula *essentia et non gradu tantum* nella dottrina cattolica sul sacerdozio." *Lateranum* 47 (1981): 98–101.

Aillet, Marc, and Guy-Marie Bagnard. *Prêtres pour le salut du monde.* Paris: Parole et Silence, 2009.

Alberigo, Giuseppe. *Les Conciles Œcuméniques: l'histoire.* Vol. 1 of *L'Histoire.* Paris: Cerf, 1994. English translation: *History of Vatican II.* 5 volumes. Maryknoll, N.Y.: Orbis, 1995–2006.

Andereggen, Ignacio. *Sacerdocio y plenitud de vida.* Buenos Aires: Pontifícia Universidad Católica de Argentina, 2004.

Astigueta, Damián Guillermo. *La noción de laico desde el Concilio Vaticano II al Codex Iuris Canonici 83.* Rome: Pontificia Università Gregoriana, 1999.

Benedict XVI and Robert Sarah. *From the Depths of Our Hearts. Priesthood, Celibacy, and the Crisis of the Catholic Church.* San Francisco: Ignatius Press, 2020.

De Bertolis, Ottavio. *Origine ed esercizio della potestà ecclesiastica di governo in San Tammaso*. Rome: Pontificia Università Gregoriana, 2005.

Betti, Umberto. *La dottrina sull'episcopato del Concilio Vaticano II*. Rome: Pontificio Ateneo Antonianum, 1984.

Blot, Thierry. *Le curé, Pasteur, des origines à la fin du XXe siècle*. Paris: Pierre Téqui, 2000.

Boni, Andrea. *Attualità del celibato sacerdotale*. Casale Monferrato: Portalupi Editore, 2003.

Bonivento, Cesare. *Il celibato sacerdotale: istituzione ecclesiastica o tradizione apostolica?*. Cinisello Balsamo: San Paolo, 2007.

Borgonovo, Graziano. *Giovanni Paolo II e la formazione sacerdotale*. Siena: Cantagalli, 2007.

Bourgeois, Daniel. "L'unique sacerdoce de Jésus-Christ, le sacerdoce des baptisés et le sacerdoce ministériel." *Communio* 128 (November–December 1996): 15–32.

Brannen, Brett. *To Save a Thousand Souls. A Guide for Discerning a Vocation to Diocesan Priesthood*. Valdosta, Ga.: Vianney Vocations, 2016.

Cajiao, Silvio. "Le sacerdoce ministériel dans les documents de l'Église du Concile de Trente à Vatican II." Congregation for the Clergy, June 27, 2003. Accessed September 13, 2021. www.clerus.org/clerus/dati/2003-07/28-13/03SMFRA.html.

Cardoso Sobrinho, José. *Perguntas e respostas sobre o celibato sacerdotal*. Recife, Brazil: Edição do Autor, 2005. English translation: *Questions and Answers on Priestly Celibacy*. Recife, Brazil: J. Cardoso Sobrinho, 2008.

Carpin, Attilio. *Il sacramento dell'ordine. Dalla teologia isidoriana alla teologia tomista*. Bologna: Grafiche San Ruffillo, 1988.

Castellucci, Erio. *Il ministero ordinato*. Brescia: Queriniana, 2002.

_____. "A trent'anni dal decreto *Presbyterorum ordinis*. La discussione teologica post-conciliare sul ministero presbiterale." *Scuola Cattolica* 124 (1996): 3–68 and 195–264.

Cattaneo, Arturo. *Il presbiterio della chiesa particolare*. Milan: Giuffrè Editore, 1993.

Cencini, Amedeo. *Quando la carne è debole*, Milan: Paoline, 2004.

Chantraine, Georges. "L'un et l'autre sacrament." *Communio* 128 (November–December 1996): 9–14.

Chapelle, Albert. *Pour la vie du monde. Le sacrement de l'ordre*. Brussels: Institut d'Études Théologiques, 1978.

Cochini, Christian. *The Apostolic Origins of Priestly Celibacy*. San Francisco: Ignatius, 1990.

Comissão Episcopal Vocações e Ministérios. *Dicionário de orientação vocacional*. Prior Velho: Paulinas, 2008.

Commission Épiscopale du Clergé et des Séminaires. "Les prêtres dans la pensée de Vatican II." *Vocation* 233 (January –March 1966).

Confoy, Maryanne. *Religious Life and Priesthood*. New York: Paulist Press, 2008.

Congar, Yves. "Sur la trilogie: Prophète-Roi-Prêtre." *Revue des Sciences Philosophiques et Théologiques* 67, no. 1 (1983): 97–115.

Congregation for the Clergy. *Sacerdoti, forgiatori di santi per il nuovo millennio.* Vatican City: Libreria Editrice Vaticana, 2004.

Connor, Charles. *Meditations on the Catholic Priesthood.* New York: Saint Pauls, 2005.

Cordes, Paul Josef. *Inviati a servire. Presbyterorum ordinis. Storia, esegesi, temi, sistematica.* Casale Monferrato: Piemme, 1990.

_____. *Why Priests? Answers Guided by the Teaching of Benedict XVI.* New York: Scepter, 2010.

Couto, António. *Dom e carisma de ser padre.* Prior Velho: Paulinas, 2008.

Dupuy, Michel. *Bérulle et le sacerdoce. Étude historique et doctrinale. Textes inédits.* Paris: Lethielleux, 1969.

Duval, Léon Etienne, et al., *L'Église: Constitution "Lumen gentium." Texte conciliaire: introduction, commentaires.* Paris: Mame, 1965.

Esquerda Bifet, Juan. *Resurgir sacerdotal antes del Concilio Vaticano II.* Burgos: Adelcoa, 1973.

Faggioli, Massimo. *Il vescovo e il Concilio: modelo episcopale e aggiornamento al Vaticano II.* Bologna: Il Mulino, 2005.

Favale, Agostino. *Il ministero presbiterale. Aspetti dottrinali, pastorali, spirituali.* Rome: Pontificio Ateneo Salesiano, 1989.

Fiores, Stefano, and Salvatore Meo, eds. *Nuovo Dizionario di Mariologia.* Cinisello Balsamo: San Paolo, 1986.

Forte, Bruno. *Sul sacerdozio ministeriale.* Milan: Edizioni Paoline, 1989.

_____. *The Church: Icon of the Trinity. A Brief Study.* Boston: Pauline Books, 1991.

Galot, Jean. *Theology of the Priesthood.* San Francisco: Ignatius Press, 1984.

Gandin, Oswaldo. *A participação dos presbíteros na missão apostólica.* Rome: Atteneo Romano della Santa Croce, 1991.

Ghirlanda, Gianfranco. "Episcopato e presbiterato nella Lumen Gentium." *Communio* 59 (1981): 53–70.

Giblet, Jean. "Les prêtres." *Unam sanctam* 51c (1966): 914–41.

Gilson, Georges. *Les prêtres.* Paris: Desclée, 1990.

Gozzelino, Giorgio. *Nel nome del Signore. Teologia del ministero ordinato.* Turin: Elle Di Ci, 1992.

Grelot, Pierre. *Une lecture de l'Épître aux hébreux.* Paris: Cerf, 2003.

Greshake, Gisbert. *Essere preti in questo tempo.* Brescia: Queriniana, 2008.

Guarinelli, Stefano. *Il celibato dei preti: perchè sceglierlo ancora?* Milan: Paoline, 2008.

Hünermann, Peter. *Symboles et définitions de la foi catholique.* Paris: Cerf, 1996. Latest English edition: Heinrich Denzinger. *Compendium of Creeds, Definitions, and Declarations on Matters of Faith and Morals.* Edited by Peter Hunermann, Robert Fastiggi, and Anne Englund Nash. 43rd ed. San Francisco: Ignatius Press, 2012.

Jeammet, Nicole. *Le célibat pour Dieu – Regard psychanalytique*. Paris: Cerf, 2009.

Jedin, Hubert. *Il Concilio di Trento ha creato l'immagine-modello del prete?* Milan: Ancora, 1975. English translation: *A History of the Council of Trent*. Translated by Ernest Graf. St. Louis: Herder, 1957.

Kasper, Walter. *Servitori della gioia*. Brescia: Queriniana, 2007.

Kloppenburg, Boaventura. "Votes et derniers amendements de la constitution." *Unam sanctam* 51b (1966): 121–57.

Lanzetta, Serafino. *Il sacerdozio di Maria nella teologia cattolica del XX secolo. Analisi storico-teologica*. Rome: Edizione dell'Autore, 2006.

Le Guillou, Marie-Joseph. "La vocation missionnaire de l'Église." *Unam sanctam* 51b (1966): 680–98.

Lecomte, Bernard. *Jean-Paul II*. Paris: Gallimard, 2003.

Lécuyer, Joseph. *Il sacerdozio di Cristo e della Chiesa*. Bologna: Dehoniane, 1965.

_____. *Le sacrement de l'ordination. Recherche historique et théologique*. Paris: Beauchesne, 1983.

Lemaître, Franck. "Le prêtre selon Jean-Paul II." *Lumière et Vie* 257 (January–March 2003): 71–80.

Malnati, Ettore. *I ministeri nella Chiesa*. Milan: Paoline, 2008.

Matura, Thaddée. "Le célibat dans le Nouveau Testament d'après l'exégèse récente." *Nouvelle Revue Théologique* 97, no. 6 (1975): 481–500.

Maloko-Mana, Bafuidinsoni. *Le "munus regendi" de l'évêque diocésain comme "munus patris et pastoris" selon le Concile Vatican II*. Rome: Pontificia Università Gregoriana, 1999.

Marini, Mario. *Le célibat sacerdotal: Forme de vie apostolique avec des textes de Benoît XVI et Jean-Paul II*. Condé-sur-Noireau: Le Forum, 2006.

Mezzadri, Luigi. *A lode e gloria. Il sacerdozio nell'École Française*. Milan: Jaca Book, 1989.

Müller, Hubert. "De differentia inter episcopatum et presbyteratum iuxta doctrina Concilii Vaticani II." *Periodica de re morali canonica liturgica* 59 (1970): 598–618.

Nascentes dos Santos, Tarsicio. "Introdução ao discurso antropológico de João Paulo II." Dissertation. Rome: Pontificio Ateneo della Santa Croce, 1992.

Piolanti, Antonio. *I sacramenti*. Vatican City: Libreria Editrice Vaticana, 1990.

Pinheiro Teixeira, João António. *Sempre a começar, nunca a terminar: O Seminário na vida da Igreja*. Prior Velho: Paulinas, 2008.

Rahner, Karl. *La gerarchia nella Chiesa: Commento al capitolo III di Lumen gentium*. Brescia: Morcelliana, 2008.

Ruini, Camillo. *Le prêtre époux de l'Église*. Allocution June 19, 1996.

Salachas, Dimitrios. *Teologia e disciplina dei sacramenti nei codici latino e orientale*. Bologna: Edizioni Dehoniane, 1999.

Sapienza, Leonardo. *L'amore più grande: eucaristia e sacerdozio: lettere di Giovanni Paolo II ai sacerdoti per il Giovedì Santo*. Rome: Editrice Rogate, 2005.

Saraiva Martins, José. *Il sacerdozio ministeriale*. Rome: Pontificia Università Urbaniana, 1991.

Sartore, Domenico. "Premesse alla lettura di LG 10. Annotazioni su alcuni sviluppi del Magistero ecclesiastico." *Lateranum* 47 (1981): 80–86.

Selin, Gary. *Priestly Celibacy: Theological Foundations*. Washington, D.C.: The Catholic University of America Press, 2016.

Sesboüé, Bernard. *Les Signes du Salut*. Vol. 3 of *Histoire des Dogmes*. Paris: Desclée, 1994.

De Smedt, Émile-Joseph. "Le sacerdoce des fidèles." *Unam sanctam* 51b (1966): 411–24.

Strathmann, Hermann. *L'Épître aux hébreux*. Geneva: Labor et Fides, 1989.

Szczesny, Ryszard. *La dottrina del Vaticano II sul celibato sacerdotale*. Rome: Pontificia Università Lateranense, 1986.

Testa, Benedetto. *I sacramenti della Chiesa*. Milan: Jaca Book, 2001.

Toups, David. *Reclaiming Our Priestly Character*. Omaha: IPF Publications, 2008.

Touze, Laurent. *Célibat sacerdotal et théologie nuptiale de l'ordre*. Rome: Pontificia Università della Santa Croce, 2002.

Van Leeuwen, Bertulf. "La participation universelle à la fonction prophétique du Christ." *Unam sanctam* 51b (1966): 425–55.

Vanhoye, Albert. *Old Testament Priests and the New Priest According to the New Testament*. Petersham, Mass.: Saint Bede's Publications, 1986.

_____. *Vivere nella Nuova Alleanza*. Rome: Edizioni ADP, 1995.

_____. *Cristo sommo sacerdote della Nuova Alleanza*. Treviso: Editrice San Liberale, 2002.

_____. *La lettre aux hébreux*. Paris: Desclée, 2002.

Verlinde, Joseph-Marie. *Prêtres pour le troisième millénaire: spiritualité sacerdotale à l'école de Jean-Paul II*. Versailles: Saint-Paul, 2001.

Villemin, Laurent. *Pouvoir d'ordre et pouvoir de juridiction*. Paris: Cerf, 2003.

Vilnet, Jean. "Orientations doctrinales du Concile." *Vocation* 233 (January 1966): 224–31.

Viscome, Francesco. *Origine ed esercizio della potestà dei vescovi dal Vaticano I al Vaticano II*. Rome: Pontificia Università Gregoriana, 1997.

Wasselynck, René. *Les prêtres. Elaboration du décret "Presbyterorum ordinis" de Vatican II*. Paris: Desclée, 1968.

Weigel, George. *Witness to Hope: The Biography of Pope John Paul II*. New York: Harper Perennial, 1999.

Witte, Jean-Louis. "L'Église *sacramentum unitatis* du cosmos et du genre humain." *Unam sanctam* 51b (1966): 457–91.

Appendix

Selected Homilies and Address of John Paul II

While this book refers to the letters to priests of John Paul II that can be read in the book *Letters to My Brother Priests* (Downers Grove, IL: Midwest Theological Forum, 2006), among the addresses and homilies not included there, I have chosen three to conclude this book: two homilies and a closing reflection and prayer for the European Episcopal Conference.

CHRISM MASS HOMILY, HOLY THURSDAY, APRIL 17, 2003

1. *"By your Holy Spirit you anointed your only Son High Priest of the new and eternal covenant."*

These words that we will shortly hear in the *Preface* are *an appropriate catechesis on the Priesthood of Christ.* He is the Supreme Pontiff of future benefits, who desired to perpetuate his Priesthood in the Church through the service of ordained ministers, to whom he entrusted the task of preaching the Gospel and of celebrating the Sacraments of salvation.

This evocative celebration on Holy Thursday morning, which sees Priests gathered around the altar with their Bishop, constitutes in a certain sense an "introduction" to the holy Triduum of Easter.

During it, the Oils and Chrism are blessed which will be used for the anointing of catechumens, for the comfort of the sick, and for the conferral of Confirmation and holy Orders.

The Oils and Chrism, closely linked to the Paschal Mystery, effectively contribute to the renewal of the life of the Church through the Sacraments. The Holy Spirit, through these sacramental signs, never ceases to sanctify the Christian people.

2. *"Today this Scripture has been fulfilled in your hearing"* (Lk 4:21).

The Gospel passage just proclaimed in our assembly takes us back to the synagogue of Nazareth where Jesus, opening the scroll of Isaiah, began to read: *"The Spirit of the Lord is upon me, because he has anointed me"* (Lk 4:18). He applies the Prophet's oracle himself, concluding: *"Today this Scripture has been fulfilled"* (v. 21).

Every time the liturgical assembly gathers to celebrate the Eucharist, *this "today" is actualized.* The mystery of Christ, the single and supreme High Priest of the new and eternal Covenant, is made present and efficacious.

In this light, we understand better the value of our priestly ministry. The Apostle invites us to revive ceaselessly the gift of God received through the imposition of hands (cf. 2 Tm 1:6), sustained by the comforting certainty that the One who has begun this work in us will bring it to completion until the day of Jesus Christ (cf. Phil 1:6).

Your Eminences, venerable Brothers in the Episcopate, dear Priests, I greet you with affection. Today, with the Holy Chrism Mass, we commemorate this *great truth that directly concerns us*. Christ has called us, in a special way, to share in his Priesthood. Every vocation to the priestly ministry is an *extraordinary gift* of God's love and, at the same time, a *profound mystery* which concerns the inscrutable divine designs and the depths of the human conscience.

3. *"Forever I will sing the goodness of the Lord"* (Responsorial Psalm).

With hearts filled with gratitude, we will shortly be renewing our priestly promises. This rite takes our minds and hearts back to the unforgettable day on which we made *the commitment to be closely united to Christ*, the model of our priesthood, and to be *faithful stewards of God's mysteries*, not allowing human interest to guide us, but only love for God and our neighbor.

Dear Brothers in the priesthood, have we remained faithful to these promises? Never let the spiritual enthusiasm of priestly Ordination be extinguished within us. And you, beloved faithful, pray for priests so that they may be attentive stewards of the gifts of divine grace, especially of God's mercy in the sacrament of Confession and the Bread of life in the Eucharist, the living memorial of the death and Resurrection of Christ.

4. *"From generation to generation I will announce his truth"* (Communion Antiphon).

Every time the Eucharist Sacrifice is celebrated in the liturgical assembly, *the "truth"* of Christ's death and Resurrection *is renewed*. It is what we will do with special emotion this evening as we relive the Last Supper of the Lord. To emphasize the *timeliness of the great commemoration of redemption*, during the Mass *of the Lord's Supper* I will sign the Encyclical entitled: *Ecclesia de Eucharistia*, which I especially wanted to address to you, dear Priests, instead of my usual Letter for Holy Thursday. Accept it as special gift of the 25th anniversary of my Petrine ministry and share it with the souls entrusted to your pastoral care.

May the Virgin Mary, the Woman of the "Eucharist" who carried the incarnate Word in her womb and made herself a ceaseless offering to the Lord, lead us all to an ever deeper understanding of the immense *gift and mystery* which the Priesthood is. May she make us worthy of her Son Jesus, the Eternal High Priest. Amen!

THE CHARISM OF THE CELIBATE PRIESTHOOD IS A GIFT FOR THE PERSON AND FOR THE CHURCH: REFLECTION AND PRAYER AT THE CLOSE OF THE MEETING WITH THE PRESIDENTS OF THE EUROPEAN EPISCOPAL CONFERENCES, DECEMBER 1, 1992

At the end of this meeting, which has enabled us to deepen our communion and ecclesial solidarity, I would like to share with you some *reflections* in connection with the 1990 Synod of Bishops, and then conclude with a *prayer* entrusting to the Lord all our pastoral concerns, in particular the commitment of those who share with us in the priesthood, and their fidelity to the call to serve the kingdom of God with total dedication.

I. Reflection

Christ's words concerning celibacy for the sake of the kingdom of heaven are coupled with the explanation that he offers to the Apostle: "Not all can receive this saying, but only those to whom it is given" (Mt 19:11). As the Gospel presents it, celibacy is a gift for the individual and, in him and through him, a gift for the Church.

The 1990 Synod of Bishops invited us once again to reaffirm the value of this gift and expressed once more the desire that it should remain an inheritance of the Latin Church for the good of her mission. This was duly expressed in the Post-Synodal Exhortation *Pastores dabo vobis*. That document contains a synthesis of the statements of the Synod Fathers and quotes its final proposals. Those who took part in the Synod cannot forget the testimonies given by individual Bishops from all over the world regarding the great value of priestly celibacy. These testimonies largely gave the Synod its "tone."

All this should give rise to faith and trust that *the One who began this good work in us will bring it to completion* (cf. Phil 1:6). What is needed on our part, then, is full confidence in the divine Giver of spiritual gifts. This confidence is especially important in places where the Church is exposed to the risk of a special challenge with regard to vocations. It is often hard to avoid the impression that a specific strategy is at work which has as one of its aims to distance the Church from fidelity to her Lord and Spouse.

But Christ himself is faithful to his covenant and *he has the power to work through the Holy Spirit*, who makes it possible to overcome the spirit of this world and to see celibacy for sake of the kingdom of God as a choice of life, against all human weakness and human strategies. *We only need not to lose heart*, or to create around this vocation and choice a climate of discouragement. The Catholic Church esteems other traditions, especially those of the Churches of the East, but she wishes to remain faithful to the charism which she has received and embraced as a gift from her Lord and Master. This fidelity and ardent prayer will open the way to the priesthood even in the most unfavorable conditions.

I am writing these words in connection with the Exhortation *Pastores dabo vobis*. At the same time they represent a heartfelt appeal to the whole Church, and in a particular way to her Pastors. The centuries-old tradition confirmed by the Second Vatican Council and by the subsequent Synods, especially the last one devoted to priestly formation, requires all of us *to be faithful and to trust in the "Lord of the harvest"* (Mt 9:38).

In terms of the universal Church, the solidarity of the Bishops will make it possible to find a solution through an "exchange of gifts" between Churches suffering from a shortage of vocations and those able to offer them help. As Christ said, "By this all will know that you are my disciples, if you have love for one another" (Jn 13:35). The solidarity of the Bishops is seen precisely in this communal love which knows how to offer and how to accept a gift.

II. Prayer

"*Pastores dabo vobis.*" With these words the whole Church turns to you, who are the "Lord of the harvest," asking for workers for your harvest, which is immense (cf. Mt 9:38). Good Shepherd, you yourself once sent the first workers into your harvest. There were twelve of them. Now that nearly two millennia have passed and their message has been spread to the ends of the earth, we *feel even more urgently the need to pray* that successors to them will be raised up in our own day—and in particular that there will be a sufficient number of those who in the ministerial priesthood build up the Church by the power of the Word of God and the sacraments; those who in your name are ministers of the Eucharist, through which the Church, which is your Body, constantly grows.

We give you thanks that from the perspective of the universal Church the temporary crisis in vocations is on the way to being overcome. With great joy we are witnessing an increase in the number of vocations in different parts of the world, in the young Churches, but also in many countries with a centuries-long Christian tradition, as well as in places where in our own century the Church has suffered various forms of persecution. With special fervor we make our prayer as we think about those societies dominated by a climate of secularization, *in which the spirit of this world hinders the action of the Holy Spirit,* so that the seed sown in the hearts of the young either does not take root or does not grow. For these societies, especially, we pray all the more: "Send forth your Spirit and renew the face of the earth."

The Church thanks you, O divine Spouse, because from the most ancient of times it has been able to welcome the call to consecrated celibacy for the sake of the kingdom of God, and because for centuries she has preserved within herself the charism of priestly celibacy. We thank you for the Second Vatican Council and for the recent Synod of Bishops which reaffirmed this charism and have shown it to be the correct way forward for the Church of the future. We are aware of the fragility of the vessels in which we carry this treasure, yet we believe in the power of the Holy Spirit who works through the grace of the sacrament in each one of us. With all the more fervor we ask you *to enable us to cooperate unfailingly with the power of the Spirit.*

We ask you, the Spirit of Christ the Good Shepherd, that we may remain faithful to this particular inheritance of the Latin Church. "Do not quench the Spirit" (1 Thes 5:19), the Apostle tells us. We pray that we may not fall into doubt or sow doubt in others or become—God forbid! —supporters of different choices and of a different kind of spirituality for the priestly life and ministry. For Saint Paul also says, "Do not grieve the Holy Spirit of God" (Eph 4:30).

Pastores dabo vobis!

We ask you to forgive all our failings regarding this holy ministry which is your priesthood in our life. We ask you to enable us to work together perseveringly in this great harvest, *to enable us to do everything necessary to awaken vocations and guide them to maturity.* We ask you above all to help us to pray without ceasing. For you yourself said, "Pray therefore the Lord of the harvest to send out laborers into his harvest" (Mt 9:38).

When confronted with this world, which in many ways shows its indifference to the kingdom of God, may we be accompanied by the certitude which you, the Good Shepherd, poured into the hearts of the Apostles. "Be of good cheer, I have overcome the world" (Jn 16:33). This is—in spite of everything—the same world which your Father so loved that he gave you, his only-begotten Son (cf. Jn 3:16).

O Mother of the divine Son, Mother of the Church, Mother of all peoples, pray with us! Pray for us!

CHRISM MASS HOMILY, HOLY THURSDAY, APRIL 16, 1981

1. "Today this Scripture has been fulfilled in your hearing" (Lk 4:21).
Venerable and dear Brothers!

The time that passed, in Jesus Christ's life, from the day on which he spoke these words in the Synagogue of Nazareth for the first time, to the day on which he started to carry in himself the supreme mission of the Anointed, was not too long.

Christ, the Anointed: the One who comes in the fullness of the Spirit of the Lord, as the prophet Isaiah said of him: "The Spirit of the Lord God is upon me, because the Lord has anointed me. . . ; he has sent me. . ." (Is 61:1).

And now the Anointed or the One sent is at the end of his earthly mission.

The hours of these dreadful and at the same time holy days are already striking, in the course of which the Church accompanies, every year, by means of faith and the liturgy, his last Passing, *Pascha Domini*. The Church does so, finding in Him, ever anew, the beginning of the life of the Spirit and of Truth, of the Life that was to be revealed only through death. Everything that had preceded this death of the Anointed was only a preparation for this unique Pasch.

2. We, too, have gathered today, in the morning hours of Holy Thursday, to prepare for Easter.

The Cardinals and the Bishops, the Priests and the Deacons, together with the Bishop of Rome, celebrate the Liturgy of the blessing of the Chrism, of the Oil of Catechumens, and of the Oil of the sick. The morning Liturgy on Holy Thursday constitutes the annual preparation for the Pasch of Christ, communicating to everyone that fullness of the Holy Spirit, which is in himself communicating to everyone the fullness of his Anointing.

Christians are *uncti ex Uncto*!

We have met here, in conformity with the character of our ministry, to prepare the Pasch of Christ in the Church: to prepare the Pasch of the Church in each of those who take part in her mission, from the baby just born to the old man, seriously ill, who is approaching the end of his life. Each one takes part in the mission given to the whole Church by the Father, the Son and the Holy Spirit, a mission brought forth thanks to the paschal mystery of Jesus Christ.

Anointing and mission are characteristic of the whole People of God. We have come to prepare the Pasch of the Church, from which the anointing and the mission of the whole People of God begins, ever anew.

"To him who loves us and has freed us from our sins by his blood and made us a kingdom, priests to his God and Father, to him be glory and dominion for ever and ever" (Rv 1:5–6).

3. And here we are together, in the community of concelebration. We are together, the humble worshippers and unworthy administrators of the paschal mystery of Jesus Christ.

We, servants of the unceasing Pasch of the Church, chosen by the grace of God.

We are present to renew the vivifying bond of our priesthood with the one Priest, with the eternal Priest, with him "who has made us a kingdom, priests to his God and Father" (Rv 1:6).

We are present to prepare to descend together with him into the "abyss of passion," which opens together with the *Triduum Sacrum*, to bring out of this abyss again the sense of our unworthiness and infinite gratitude for the gift which is shared by each of us.

We are here, dear Brothers, to renew the vows of our priestly faithfulness: "Moreover it is required of stewards that they be found trustworthy" (1 Cor 4:2).

We are *Uncti ex Uncto*!

We have been anointed, like all our Brothers and Sisters, in the grace of Baptism and of Confirmation.

But, in addition to that, our hands have also been anointed, with which we must renew His own Sacrifice on so many altars, of this Basilica, of the Eternal City, of the whole world.

Our heads also are anointed, since the Holy Spirit has chosen some of us and has called us to preside over the Church, with apostolic solicitude for all the Churches (*sollicitudo omnium ecclesiarum*).

Uncti ex Uncto!

How priceless this day is for us! How special is today's feast: the day on which we were all and each of us born as ministerial priests thanks to the Divine Anointed.

"You shall be called the priests of the Lord; men shall speak of you as the ministers of our God" (Is 61:6).

The Lord speaks as follows: "I will faithfully give them their recompense, and I will make an everlasting covenant with them. Their descendants shall be known among the nations, and their offspring in the midst of the peoples, all who see them shall acknowledge them, that they are a people whom the Lord has blessed" (Is 61:8–9).

So the prophet Isaiah expresses himself in the first Reading.

Beloved Brothers! May these words be fulfilled in each of you and in all people.

Let us pray also for those who have broken faithfulness to their covenant with the Lord and to the anointing of the priest's hands.

Let us pray thinking of those who, after us, must assume the Anointing and the Mission. May they arrive from various directions and enter the Vineyard of the Lord, without delaying and without looking back.

Uncti ex Uncto!

Amen.

Scriptural Index

Index

Also Available from
The Catholic University of America Press

Understanding the Religious Priesthood: History, Controversy, Theology.
By Fr. Christian Raab

Priestly Celibacy: Theological Foundations.
By Fr. Gary B. Selin

A Guide to Formation Advising for Seminarians **and** *A Guide to Formation Advising for Seminary Faculty: Accompaniment, Participation, and Evaluation.*
By Deacon Edward McCormack

Called to Holiness: On Love, Vocation, and Formation.
By Pope Benedict XVI

Understanding the Diaconate: Historical, Theological, and Sociological Foundations.
By Bishop W. Shawn McKnight

Introduction to Sacramental Theology: Signs of Christ in the Flesh.
By Fr. José Granados

Bread from Heaven: An Introduction to the Theology of the Eucharist.
By Fr. Bernhard Blankenhorn

Pope John Paul II Speaks on Women.
Edited by Brooke Deely

Catechesis for the New Evangelization: Vatican II, John Paul II, and the Unity of Revelation and Experience.
By Brian Pedraza

Naming Our Sins: How Recognizing the Seven Deadly Vices Can Renew the Sacrament of Reconciliation.
Edited by Jana M. Bennett and David Cloutier